OCCASIONAL PAPER 127

Road Maps of the Transition

The Baltics, the Czech Republic, Hungary, and Russia

Biswajit Banerjee, Vincent Koen, Thomas Krueger, Mark S. Lutz, Michael Marrese, and Tapio O. Saavalainen

INTERNATIONAL MONETARY FUND
Washington DC
September 1995

Cataloging-in-Publication Data

Road maps of the transition : the Baltics, the Czech Republic, Hungary, and Russia / Biswajit Banerjee . . . [et al.]. — Washington, D.C. : International Monetary Fund, [1995]
    p. cm. — (Occasional paper, 0251-6365 ; 127)

ISBN 1-55775-519-1

1. Europe, Eastern — Economic policy — 1989– 2. Economic stabilization — Europe, Eastern. 3. Europe, Eastern — Economic conditions — 1989– I. Banerjee, Biswajit. II. Series: Occasional paper (International Monetary Fund) ; no. 127.
HB244.R63   1995

Price: US$15.00
(US$12.00 to full-time faculty members and
students at universities and colleges)

Please send orders to:
International Monetary Fund, Publication Services
700 19th Street, N.W., Washington, D.C. 20431, U.S.A.
Tel.: (202) 623-7430   Telefax: (202) 623-7201
Internet: publications@imf.org

recycled paper

Contents

Tables

Charts

The following symbols have been used throughout this paper:

... to indicate that data are not available;

— to indicate that the figure is zero or less than half the final digit shown, or that the item does not exist;

– between years or months (e.g., 1991–92 or January–June) to indicate the years or months covered, including the beginning and ending years or months;

/ between years (e.g., 1991/92) to indicate a crop or fiscal (financial) year.

"Billion" means a thousand million.

Minor discrepancies between constituent figures and totals are due to rounding.

The term "country," as used in this paper, does not in all cases refer to a territorial entity that is a state as understood by international law and practice; the term also covers some territorial entities that are not states, but for which statistical data are maintained and provided internationally on a separate and independent basis.

Preface

This collection of papers analyzes the process of transition to a market economy in the Baltic countries, the Czech Republic, Hungary, and Russia. These studies were prepared by economists of the European I and European II Departments of the IMF and incorporate their experience with these countries through early 1995.

Earlier versions of these contributions were presented in January 1995 in two panels sponsored by the Association for Comparative Economic Studies in the context of the annual meetings of the Allied Social Sciences Association. The papers on the Baltic countries and on Russia were delivered in the panel "Economic Diversity and Evolution Among States of the Former Soviet Union and the Baltic Countries," chaired by Thomas A. Wolf of the European II Department of the IMF. The discussants were Donal Donovan (IMF), Herb Levine (Pennsylvania University), and Ben Slay (Middlebury College). The papers on the Czech Republic and Hungary were delivered in the panel "Economic Success in Central and Eastern Europe," chaired by Michael Marrese. The discussants were Gerárd Bélanger (IMF), Josef Brada (Arizona State University), and David Kemme (University of Memphis). The authors are grateful to the discussants and to the other participants in those sessions for their comments. They also acknowledge valuable contributions from a number of IMF colleagues. Juanita Roushdy of the External Relations Department edited the manuscripts and coordinated production of the publication, and Alicia Etchebarne-Bourdin and the IMF Graphics Section provided composition and artwork.

The views expressed in these papers, as well as any errors, are the sole responsability of the authors and should not be construed as those of the national authorities, Executive Directors of the IMF, or other members of the IMF staff.

1 Stabilization in the Baltic Countries: Early Experience

Tapio O. Saavalainen

In mid-1992, each of the Baltic countries adopted comprehensive stabilization and reform programs. Economic conditions were very difficult; real output was falling sharply, and prices were soaring. To a large extent, these developments reflected inherited macroeconomic imbalances and supply disturbances as suggested by a strong negative correlation between real output and inflation (Chart 1.1). The final collapse of Soviet central planning in 1990–91—a systemic shock—caused widespread disruptions in trade and in financial links, which led to shortages of goods and raw materials, loss of export markets, disfunctioning of payments and monetary arrangements, and a "wait-and-see" attitude among enterprise managers. On the demand side, rising prices severely cut households' real balances, while price liberalization started to reduce queues and shortages. In 1991, the first year the effects of the systemic shock were truly felt, real net material product in the Baltic countries declined by around 10 percent. At the same time, consumer prices rose 210 percent in Estonia, 124 percent in Latvia, and 225 percent in Lithuania. As a result, those holding cash and savings deposits were severely penalized. In Estonia, for example, the stock of cash and savings deposits held by households lost about 75 percent of its real value between 1989 and 1991.[1]

Economic difficulties were aggravated in early 1992 as Estonia, Latvia, and Lithuania faced a serious terms of trade shock. Russia moved to world market prices for fuel exports to the Baltic countries and initiated a price liberalization process that increased prices of its exported raw materials and intermediate inputs. In all three Baltic countries, the

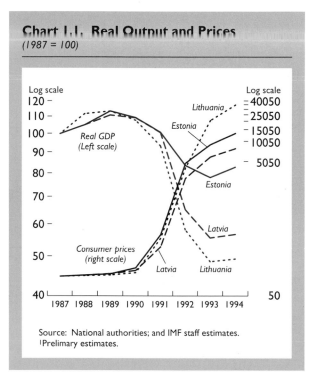

Chart 1.1. Real Output and Prices
(1987 = 100)

Source: National authorities; and IMF staff estimates.
[1]Prelimary estimates.

terms of trade deteriorated by 30–40 percent, or by 10–15 percent of GDP, while domestic price increases reached magnitudes of 50 percent or more a month.[2] Owing to their strong dependency on trade with Russia and other states of the former Soviet Union, the Baltic countries experienced a much higher terms of trade deterioration than did the Eastern European countries with the dissolution of the trade system of the Council for Mutual Economic Assistance (CMEA) and the move to spot prices from traditional reference prices in their trade

Note: An earlier version of this paper was presented at the 1995 Annual Meetings of the Allied Social Science Associations, Washington, D.C., January 6, 1995. Useful comments on earlier drafts of this paper were provided by Messrs. Thomas Wolf, Adalbert Knöbl, Leif Hansen, Adam Bennett, Michael Marrese, Ratna Sahay, and colleagues in the Baltic Division of the European II Department of the IMF. Linda Galantin and Mandana Dehghanian provided valuable research assistance. The findings and interpretations presented here, however, are the author's responsibility.

[1]In fact, the effective stock of household real balances declined even more as Russia blocked the savings accounts of the Savings Banks held by the Baltic countries in Moscow, in 1991.

[2]In January–February 1992, prices rose on average by 80 percent in Estonia, by 57 percent in Latvia, and 48 percent in Lithuania. For the terms of trade loss estimates for the Baltic countries, see Tarr (1993).

with the countries of the former Soviet Union. For example, in Poland, Hungary, and the former Czechoslovakia the terms of trade shock in 1991 ranged between 3 percent and 5$\frac{1}{2}$ percent of GDP.[3]

Under these conditions, there was little scope for a gradualist approach in policy response. In particular, the terms of trade shock and high inflation during the first half of 1992 called for rapid action to avoid a prolonged decline in output.[4] A delayed response to these problems could have led to renewed government intervention with a high likelihood of increasing political resistance to market-based reforms. In addition, the newly regained independence from the former U.S.S.R. and the strong political will to rapidly re-establish historical links to Western Europe worked against a gradualist response to the economic difficulties.

Baltic Stabilization Policies

The Baltic stabilization and reform programs were built on common cornerstones. To realign domestic prices with world prices was the most urgent task. For this, all three programs incorporated rapid completion of price and trade liberalization. To insulate themselves from inflationary impulses from the former U.S.S.R., the Baltic countries introduced their own currencies early in their programs; this enabled them to aim at price stability by pursuing sovereign monetary and exchange rate policies. Their budgetary processes became independent from the Soviet budget system as early as in 1991, and in their stabilization programs, fiscal policies were geared toward balanced budgets to prevent inflationary deficit financing. In addition, a series of structural measures aimed at institution building and rationalization of economic incentive structures were implemented.

Choice of Monetary and Exchange Rate Regime

Initially, the major difference between the three countries in their approach to stabilization was their monetary and exchange rate regimes. The small size of their economies and a strong will to re-integrate into Europe suggested an open trade regime with strong external competitiveness. It was not clear, however, whether this could be achieved better with

flexible or fixed exchange rates. The Baltic economies were prone to severe rigidities, inherited from the Soviet planning system. For example, minimum wages—and through this, other nominal wages and social benefits—were strongly linked to price increases, the inertia of which was intensified by high inflation expectations reflecting past experience. Therefore, to improve discipline in price and wage setting, as well as in fiscal management, the setting of an anchor for nominal magnitudes argued for the adoption of a fixed exchange rate regime. Also, having already experienced a severe terms of trade shock, the most likely shocks expected to occur, at least in the short run were to be monetary in nature, which suggested fixing the exchange rate for monetary discipline.[5]

These arguments had to be balanced against the view that with a fixed exchange rate the Baltic countries would be more exposed to external shocks—further oil price increases, economic and political disturbances in Russia, exchange rate changes in neighboring countries, and so on—than under a flexible exchange rate regime. In addition, a factor favoring a floating rate regime was the recent experience with high price increases and obvious high inflation expectations; a flexible rate could be assumed to help stabilize competitiveness.

Given these considerations, it was not surprising that the Baltic countries took diverse views in choosing their exchange rate regimes. In Estonia, the primary consideration for exchange rate policy was credibility. It was thought that the only way to drive the ruble, the Finnish markka, and U.S. dollar from circulation was to fix the exchange rate of the kroon. Merely fixing the rate, however, was not sufficient; to establish full credibility, the currency needed the backing of assets with recognized value. For this, gold reserves became available in 1992 following the agreement to repatriate gold deposited by Estonia in Western central banks before the occupation of the country in 1940. In this context, the idea of a currency board was introduced. The exchange rate for the kroon was set close to the market rate for the ruble.[6] This rate implied a monthly average wage of around $30, or about one seventh of the average wage in Poland at that time—an indication of an initial undervaluation of the exchange rate. The currency board arrangement, which prevented the central bank from extending credit to state enterprises, agriculture, and the government, made it easier to resist shocks to the supply of money. The money

---

[3]See Rodrik (1992).

[4]After the terms of trade shock, but before the adoption of the stabilization programs, average monthly inflation remained at 15 percent in Estonia, 18 percent in Latvia, and 12 percent in Lithuania.

[5]The risk of uncontrolled monetary expansion was high given the legacy of the planning economy, which maintained strong demands for special credit allocations to certain sectors (agriculture, heavy industry, and so on).

[6]The conversion rate was set at Rub 10 per kroon.

growth thereby became fully demand determined.[7] The Estonian kroon was fixed at EEK 8 per DM1, and the base money supply was fully backed by foreign reserves, initially by gold, but soon afterward by interest-bearing deutsche mark assets.

In Latvia, credibility was also important. Latvia's restituted gold reserves, however, were not as large as Estonia's, which was one factor supporting the authorities' choice of a floating exchange rate regime. Further, in May 1992, a new central bank law was introduced creating a strong, independent central bank, headed by a governor who was widely known for his strong anti-inflationary policy stance. Thus, the prospects for the implementation of tight monetary policies were considered good, in particular because such policies were supported by the government and by the majority in Parliament. It was realized from the outset that the Latvian ruble (later to become the lats) had to earn its credibility in the market through tight monetary policy. For this purpose, the central bank chose money as a nominal anchor for the price system. Tight limits for the growth of credit, and later for the monetary base, were set to strengthen foreign reserves and keep inflation under control, that is, a strict monetary rule was adopted to prevent domestic monetary shocks. As in Estonia, the Latvian currency was considered strongly undervalued. At first, it floated against foreign currencies but the float became managed in late 1992, as the Bank of Latvia began to intervene in the foreign exchange market to prevent excessive nominal appreciation. Since February 1994, the Bank of Latvia has de facto pegged its currency to the SDR; however, public commitment to a fixed rate regime has not been announced.

Lithuania was the last of the Baltic countries to leave the ruble area, and defining the exchange rate and monetary arrangements was less straightforward. The authorities' initial commitment to stabilization was less pronounced than in Estonia and Latvia, and the independence of the central bank was weak. Also, of the three Baltic states, the Lithuanian central bank had the smallest amount of foreign reserves relative to the size of the country. As a first step toward monetary sovereignty, an interim coupon currency, the talonas, was introduced in May 1992; however, it circulated in parallel and at a par with the ruble, and insulation from instability in Russia was not achieved. It was not until October 1, 1992 that the talonas was declared sole legal tender and the ruble taken out of circulation. A permanent national currency, the litas, was introduced on June 25, 1993, and on April 1, 1994 Lithuania also introduced a currency board, although initially with a lower degree of reserve backing than

Estonia's.[8] The litas was pegged against the U.S. dollar at the rate of 4 litai per U.S. dollar.

Developments in Exchange Rates and Monetary Aggregates

The confidence in the new Baltic currencies and their adopted stabilization policies was reflected in the developments of the exchange rates and foreign reserves (Chart 1.2). Estonia's nominal exchange rate began to appreciate against the ruble immediately after the currency reform, and against the U.S. dollar it moved in line with the deutsche mark/dollar cross rate, given the deutsche mark peg. As an indication of confidence in the fixed rate regime, foreign reserves began to accumulate rapidly.

In Latvia, a notable premium against the ruble began to develop in August, but the rate against the U.S. dollar stabilized only in October 1992. The delay in the stabilization against the U.S. dollar reflected the authorities' concerns about competitiveness, as the Russian ruble continued to depreciate against the dollar. With a shift of emphasis toward price stabilization, monetary policies were gradually tightened and the currency began to appreciate against the U.S. dollar. Later, with the growth of monetary aggregates slowing down to levels already prevailing in Estonia under the currency board arrangement, tight credit and high interest rates led to considerable capital inflows, accumulation of foreign reserves, and further currency appreciation. The overall money supply became endogenous with the de facto fixed exchange rate regime in February 1994. While credit policy remained tight during 1994, the appreciation of the lats against the U.S. dollar has reflected more the weakness of the dollar relative to the SDR than the stance of domestic monetary policies.

In Lithuania, monetary discipline remained weak initially as the Bank of Lithuania continued to give in to a wide spectrum of credit demands. In addition, liquidity was boosted by large ruble inflows in late 1992. As a result, the exchange rate against the Russian ruble remained broadly unchanged, and it depreciated substantially against the U.S. dollar until spring 1993. The demand for talonai declined, and currency substitution expanded. In spring 1993, the authorities estimated that some 30–50 percent of transactions were being conducted in foreign currency. The course of monetary policy was radically reversed in May by a

---

[7]For a detailed discussion on the operation of Estonia's currency board, see Bennett (1993) and (1994).

[8]While Estonia's base money was fully backed with net international reserves, in Lithuania, the cover of base money with net international reserves (gross reserves minus purchases from the IMF) remained negative initially, although it was fully covered with gross reserves.

Chart 1.2. Exchange Rates and Monetary Aggregates

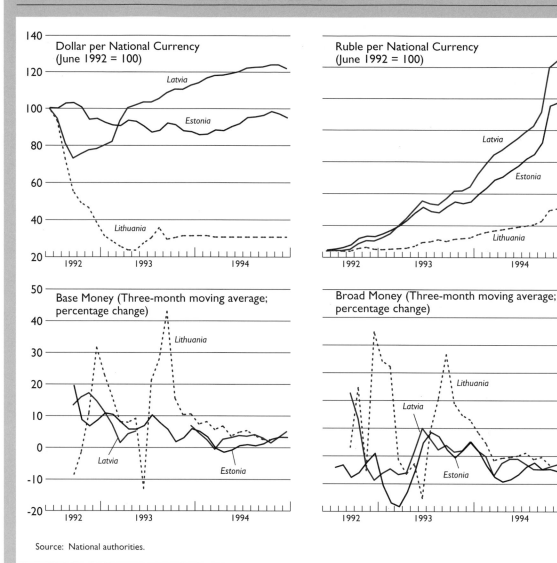

Source: National authorities.

substantial tightening of reserve requirements.[9] Monetary stabilization gained momentum, foreign reserves began to rise, and the currency appreciated against the U.S. dollar between May and August 1993. After that, the litas remained stable. In April 1994, it was anchored to the U.S. dollar by a currency board arrangement to divest the influence

of interest groups from the formulation of monetary policies.

Fiscal Policies

Tight fiscal policies were crucial to Baltic economic programs from the outset. The fiscal stance was seen as an important signal of the government's commitment to stabilization, and fiscal consolidation was aimed at bolstering confidence in the programs and lowering inflationary expectations. Through 1992 and

---

[9] Apart from raising the reserve requirement ratio from 10 percent to 12 percent, foreign currency deposits were also made subject to reserve requirement, implying a more than doubling of the effective reserve requirements.

1993, the Baltic financial balances remained broadly in balance while only more recently small deficits have developed in Latvia and Lithuania.[10] This contrasts sharply to the experience in Poland, Hungary, Russia, and other countries of the former Soviet Union where fiscal deficits were major impediments to the stabilization process (Table 1.1).

Did the Baltic countries have some comparative advantage in establishing fiscal equilibrium at the outset of the reform process, and to what extent did their fiscal management contribute to apparent fiscal prudence? One explanation appears to be that the initial fiscal position in all three Baltic countries was indeed better than in Russia and the transition economies in Central Europe, partly because of the early budget reforms in 1990–91. During the Soviet era, the Baltic countries, in particular Latvia and Lithuania, had rendered large net transfers to the all-union budget.[11] Their financial balances improved considerably with the abolition of these transfers in connection with the budget reforms. For example, a large part of Latvia's and Lithuania's swing from a fiscal deficit in 1989–90 to a surplus of 5–6 percent of GDP in 1991 can be explained by this factor.

Also, a comparison of the initial level of revenues suggests that the Baltic countries may have had a greater potential for strengthening their revenue base than the Central European countries, where revenue-to-GDP ratios were very high at the beginning of the reform process (Table 1.2).[12] Revenue levels in the Baltic countries before the reforms appear to have been about one third lower relative to GDP than in Hungary and the former Czechoslovakia, although at about the same level as in Poland.[13] The large difference between the Baltic countries and Hungary and the former Czechoslovakia was partly due to the latter's very high statutory payroll tax rates (over 50 percent in the

former Czechoslovakia and as high as 63 percent in Hungary) and higher nontax revenue collection.

Estonia and Latvia, in particular, took the opportunity to augment tax revenues early on. Indeed, after declining in 1992, their revenue-to-GDP ratios rose in 1993, the first full year with stabilization programs, while the decline continued in Lithuania. In Estonia, a strong revenue package amounting to 5–6 percent of GDP was introduced to support the currency reform in mid-1992. The value-added tax (VAT) rate was raised from 10 percent to 18 percent, and the tax rates on corporate and personal incomes were increased. Later, increases were decreed on excise taxes. As a result, the collection of indirect taxes relative to GDP returned to the prereform level. Moreover, payroll taxation had been increased in early 1992 by introducing a new medical tax at a rate of 13 percent of wage earnings. In addition, tax scales were not fully adjusted to compensate for inflation, thus, personal income tax collection was higher in 1993 than before the reform. Revenue from corporate taxation, however, declined relative to GDP, which mainly reflected the initial increase in tax arrears, falling profitability in state enterprises, and the difficulty in collecting taxes from the emerging private sector.

In Latvia, new tax measures were delayed to late 1992. Thereafter, the VAT rate was raised first from 10 percent to 12 percent, and further to 18 percent in October, 1993, while administration of this tax was greatly improved. Similarly, excise taxes were increased on several occasions. As a result, the share of indirect taxes in GDP increased despite the fact that the tax base (mainly private consumption) fell more rapidly than nominal GDP in 1993. Profit taxes remained surprisingly resilient to the output fall, owing to highly profitable re-exports of goods from the countries of the former Soviet Union. Payroll taxes were buoyant, owing to a change in the shares of factor incomes in favor of wages as employment fell less than real GDP.

Among the Baltic countries, but also in comparison with Central Europe, Lithuania faced the largest shortfall in revenues. Unlike in other Baltic countries, no turnaround in revenue ratios took place in 1993, and the tax ratio declined to about 10 percentage points below that in Estonia and Latvia. The major factor contributing to this decline was a marked adjustment in the distribution of factor incomes away from wages. With differentiated tax treatment of profits and labor, the shift is estimated to have contributed to the decline in the revenue-to-GDP ratio by one third to one half.[14] The fall in the share of indirect taxes to GDP was due largely to a decline in consumption relative to GDP as real wages declined

---

[10]In their first programs (from mid-1992 to mid-1993), Estonia and Lithuania aimed at balanced budgets (measured by the financial balance, i.e., overall fiscal balance minus net lending), despite a large expected fall in economic activity, while Latvia's program allowed for a small deficit (1–2 percent of GDP). In their second programs (mid-1993 to the end of 1994), all three countries allowed a small (1–2 percent of GDP) financial deficit, mainly to accommodate unexpected expenditure pressures (such as a higher-than-expected rise in unemployment benefits) or revenue shortfalls.

[11]In Latvia, this net transfer was estimated to have reached 14 percent of GDP in 1988 and 1989, and in Lithuania about 6 percent of GDP in 1989–90 on average. Estonia, though, had already reduced its net transfers from earlier, higher levels to some 2 percent of GDP by 1989.

[12]Inferences based on GDP estimates here and elsewhere in the paper must be treated with a great deal of caution given the well-known measurement problems as regards national accounts in the former planned economies.

[13]Prereform comparisons for Central Europe are for 1989 and for the Baltic countries, 1991.

[14]See IMF (1994).

Table 1.1. Fiscal Balances[1]
(In percent of GDP)

	1989	1990	1991	1992	1993	1994
Estonia						
Financial balance[2]	...	...	5.2	0.8	1.4	0.9
Fiscal balance	...	...	5.2	0.2	0.7	—
Latvia						
Financial balance[2]	...	...	6.3	—	1.0	−1.7
Fiscal balance	...	...	6.4	−0.8	0.6	−4.1
Lithuania						
Financial balance[2]	...	...	4.6	0.8	1.4	−1.9
Fiscal balance	...	...	2.5	0.9	−4.0	−4.7
Russia						
Fiscal balance[2]	...	...	−16.0	−18.8	−8.0	...
Poland						
Financial balance[3]	−7.3	3.2	−6.5	−6.7	−2.9	...
Hungary						
Financial balance[4]	−1.7	0.5	−2.1	−5.5	−6.7	...
Czechoslovakia, former						
Financial balance[4]	−2.7	0.1	−1.9	−3.6	...	...

Sources: National authorities; and IMF staff estimates.
[1] Financial balance is defined as overall fiscal balance (using *Government Finance Statistics* methodology) minus net lending.
[2] On a cash basis.
[3] On a commitment basis, except external interest payments are on a cash basis.
[4] On a commitment basis.

sharply. In addition, it appears that the efficiency of tax collection in Lithuania has lagged behind that in other Baltic countries, as suggested by higher tax arrears and the fact that the share of profit taxes of GDP continued to decline despite the shift in functional distribution of income in favor of profits.

The structure and management of public expenditures also contributed to the good fiscal performance in the Baltic countries (Table 1.3). First, given the initial surplus in the fiscal accounts and better revenue performance, it was easier to implement strict cash rationing as a tool for expenditure control compared with Central European countries with initial fiscal deficits. Tight cash rationing has effectively controlled spending on nonpriority areas (mainly purchases of goods and services) but also in local governments and social security funds, which to a large extent have been dependent on central government budget transfers in financing their outlays. In addition, central bank credit to finance government expenditures has been eliminated completely by institutional arrangements, as in Estonia, or it has been limited as a matter of policy, as in Latvia and in Lithuania even prior to the introduction of the currency

board in the latter. With these practices, cash rationing has worked effectively in the Baltic countries.

Another marked difference compared with the Central European countries (in particular in Estonia and Lithuania) has been the development of social security benefits. The share of these outlays, contrary to Central Europe, has remained stable in Estonia and declined in Lithuania, partly reflecting the low, officially recorded unemployment, but also tight pension policies. In Latvia, these benefits have increased faster than GDP, partly due to rising recorded unemployment; they also reflect more generous pensions and social benefits.

In Central European countries, in particular Hungary and Poland, interest payments have been higher than in the Baltic countries, reflecting high initial debt levels and further increases in interest payments stemming from the cleanup of bad loans of the state enterprises in commercial banks' balance sheets. Finally, it also appears that the Baltic governments have been more successful in reducing subsidies to very low levels, while they still made up some 2½–5 percent of GDP in Central Europe after two-to-three years of reform.

Table 1.2. General Government Revenue
(In percent of GDP)

	1989	1990	1991	1992	1993	1994[1]
Estonia						
Total revenue		. . .	41.0	33.3	39.9	34.9
Tax revenue		. . .	38.1	30.8	37.9	33.4
Corporate tax		. . .	8.4	5.6	4.8	3.0
Personal income tax		. . .	7.4	6.7	8.5	7.2
Payroll tax		. . .	8.8	9.2	12.0	10.5
VAT and excises		. . .	11.1	8.5	11.1	11.3
Latvia						
Total revenue		. . .	37.4	28.2	35.8	36.3
Tax revenue		. . .	36.5	27.9	35.4	35.4
Corporate tax		. . .	7.3	5.6	7.8	3.8
Personal income tax		. . .	3.6	2.7	3.9	4.8
Payroll tax		. . .	10.3	9.3	11.3	12.2
VAT and excises		. . .	10.1	6.5	8.7	11.8
Lithuania						
Total revenue		. . .	43.0	33.1	28.6	25.4
Tax revenue		. . .	41.5	32.1	26.6	24.7
Corporate tax		. . .	6.8	5.8	5.3	2.6
Personal income tax		. . .	5.2	5.2	5.1	5.5
Payroll tax		. . .	10.2	8.2	6.4	7.0
VAT and excises		. . .	13.9	10.8	8.0	7.3
Poland						
Total revenue	41.5	43.0	41.5	44.0	45.5	
Tax revenue	33.8	35.6	34.5	37.4	39.1	
Corporate tax	. . .	14.0	6.1	4.6	5.3	
Personal income tax	. . .	3.0	2.4	7.4	9.1	
Payroll tax	. . .	7.4	9.9	10.7	9.9	
VAT and excises	. . .	6.3	7.4	9.0	10.6	
Hungary						
Total revenue	59.2	54.0	52.2	56.1	55.5	
Tax revenue	46.4	44.6	42.3	41.5	42.1	
Corporate tax	. . .	7.0	5.3	2.5	2.0	
Personal income tax	. . .	5.7	6.9	7.7	8.1	
Payroll tax	. . .	12.8	13.1	13.7	13.5	
VAT and excises	. . .	11.4	11.5	11.9	12.4	
Czechoslovakia, former						
Total revenue	69.5	60.1	51.5	51.6	. . .	
Tax revenue	58.6	53.4	43.3	43.1	. . .	
Corporate tax	. . .	12.5	13.7	11.7	. . .	
Personal income tax	. . .	6.7	6.1	7.7	. . .	
Payroll tax	. . .	14.4	11.0	10.3	. . .	
VAT and excises	. . .	18.0	12.6	12.8	. . .	

Sources: National authorities; and IMF staff estimates.
[1] Preliminary estimates.

Stabilization Performance

Inflation

Successful financial polices have been reflected in a rapid slowdown of inflation in the Baltic countries (Chart 1.3). As in Poland and the former Czechoslovakia, the price level began to stabilize quickly after the adoption of stabilization programs in Estonia and Latvia, while it took somewhat longer in Lithuania. As portrayed in Chart 1.4, since autumn

Table 1.3. General Government Expenditure
(In percent of GDP)

	1989	1990	1991	1992	1993	1994[1]
Estonia						
Total expenditure		. . .	35.8	32.5	38.5	34.0
Goods and services		. . .	17.5	21.4	23.8	23.0
Interest payments		. . .	—	—	0.1	. . .
Social security benefits		. . .	11.7	8.0	10.6	9.0
Subsidies		. . .	2.8	1.7	1.5	0.5
Capital expenditure		. . .	3.8	1.4	2.5	1.3
Latvia						
Total expenditure		. . .	31.1	28.2	34.8	38.0
Goods and services		. . .	15.4	16.5	18.8	19.9
Interest payments		. . .	—	0.1	0.9	0.7
Social security benefits		. . .	11.4	9.8	14.0	16.1
Subsidies		. . .	1.3	0.3	—	0.2
Capital expenditure		. . .	3.0	1.5	1.1	1.1
Lithuania						
Total expenditure		. . .	38.4	32.3	27.2	27.3
Goods and services		. . .	13.6	14.8	12.1	12.8
Interest payments		. . .	—	—	—	0.1
Social security benefits		. . .	14.6	12.8	10.7	10.1
Subsidies		. . .	5.5	2.1	1.5	1.3
Capital expenditure		. . .	4.7	2.6	2.9	3.0
Poland						
Total expenditure	48.8	39.8	48.0	50.7	48.4	
Goods and services	21.4	18.7	21.9	22.6	20.3	
Interest payments	—	0.4	1.5	3.2	3.9	
Social security benefits	11.2	10.6	17.3	19.9	20.4	
Subsidies	12.9	7.3	5.1	3.3	2.3	
Capital expenditure	3.3	2.8	2.2	1.7	1.5	
Hungary						
Total expenditure	60.9	53.5	54.3	61.6	62.2	
Goods and services	25.4	23.6	20.4	23.8	28.7	
Interest payments	2.4	2.8	3.8	6.0	4.7	
Social security benefits	14.4	13.9	16.9	18.4	17.4	
Subsidies	12.1	8.9	7.5	5.6	4.3	
Capital expenditure	6.6	4.3	5.8	7.8	7.0	
Czechoslovakia, former						
Total expenditure	72.2	60.0	53.4	55.2	. . .	
Goods and services	25.2	23.5	22.5	25.0	. . .	
Interest payments	—	0.2	0.5	1.1	. . .	
Social security benefits	13.6	13.7	16.1	16.4	. . .	
Subsidies	25.0	15.7	7.6	5.2	. . .	
Capital expenditure	8.5	6.8	6.7	7.5	. . .	

Sources: National authorities; and IMF staff estimates.
[1] Preliminary estimates.

1992, the price levels in Estonia and Latvia have moved broadly in parallel with those in Poland. However, two years or so after the introduction of the stabilization programs, the monthly price increases appear to have remained stubborn at levels implying an annual rate of inflation of 20–30 percent. Similar inflation rates, and even higher, were observed in Poland where annualized monthly inflation was above 50 percent after about two years of reform. In the former Czechoslovakia, however, the

Chart 1.3. Consumer Price Index
(Three-month moving average; percentage change over preceeding month)

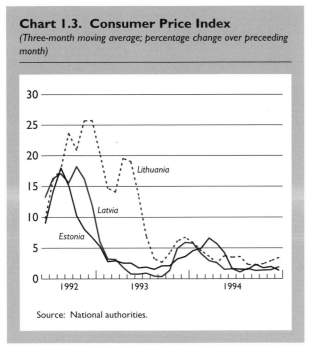

Source: National authorities.

Chart 1.4. Inflation in Baltic and Central European Countries

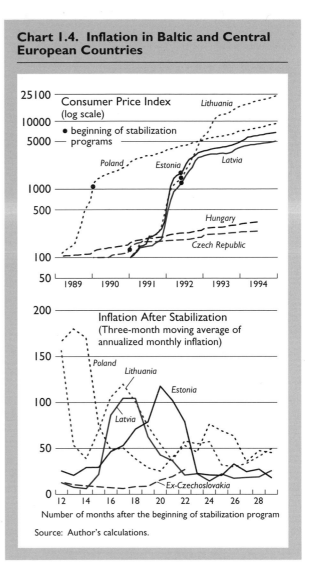

Number of months after the beginning of stabilization program

Source: Author's calculations.

monthly inflation remained lower after the reform than in the Baltic countries.[15]

Excessive wage increases do not appear to explain the price pressures in the Baltic context (Chart 1.5). The real wage adjustment has been significant in all three countries, although it took place with varying speed. At the time of the adoption of the stabilization and reform programs in mid-1992, real wages in Estonia had already declined by more than 40 percent compared with the level before the terms of trade shock. Sharp reductions, although from higher levels, took place also in Lithuania, and a further decline in real wages was called for in the beginning of the stabilization program. In Latvia, real wages have declined less, and a larger part of the adjustment took place through higher unemployment.[16] After the initial declines, the average measured real wage has remained relatively stable in each Baltic country.

---

[15]In 1994, the annualized inflation rates fell to below 10 percent in the Czech Republic, were slightly higher than 10 percent in the Slovak Republic, and hovered around 30 percent in Poland. In Hungary, the annualized rate of inflation was around 13 percent in the first three quarters of 1994.

[16]Although the official data on unemployment are not comparable with Western figures owing to definitional differences, a comparison between the Baltic countries where cross-country definitional problems are smaller indicates that Latvia's unemployment figures are higher than in Estonia and Lithuania. The access and eligibility rules in the Latvian unemployment compensation scheme appear more generous, however, than in Estonia and Lithuania, which may account for part of the differences in official unemployment figures.

Lax financial policies cannot explain the Baltic inflation, either. As discussed above, both monetary and fiscal policies have remained strict in Estonia and Latvia throughout 1993 and 1994. In Lithuania, fiscal policies have been roughly in line with those in the other two Baltic countries, and monetary discipline has been strong since mid-1993. These observations suggest two other sources of inflation: administrative price increases and exchange rate developments.

A gradual elimination of implicit subsidization has kept administered price increases high in all Baltic countries. In particular, housing rents, transportation fares, and prices of public utilities (electricity, gas, water, sewage, and so on) have risen faster than overall inflation. Pressures on rents have resulted from a low initial cost recovery ratio in rental housing, the stock of which largely remained under governmental

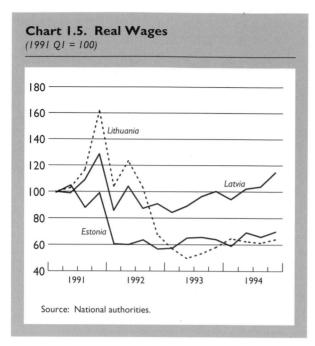

Chart 1.5. Real Wages
(1991 Q1 = 100)

Source: National authorities.

ownership, except in Lithuania. Similarly, utility prices have continued to increase faster than the general price level, reflecting remnants of cross-subsidization of households from electricity and gas companies owing to the slow breaking up of these monopolies and their lack of true incentives to rationalize their operations. In the same vein, public transportation still remains subsidized, maintaining the pressure on fares. As these structures were not dismantled at the outset of the reform, the governments have been slow in restoring full cost recovery, partly due to the inability to pay among large segments of the population.[17] With gradual improvement in the social safety net and real incomes, corrections in these prices have gathered speed and have kept actual price increases above the levels of underlying inflation.

The initial undervalued level of the real exchange rates appears to explain a large part of the Baltic inflation process. With undervaluation of the exchange rate, a free trading system, and rapid movement to current and capital account convertibility, international price arbitrage became effective in moving the prices of tradable goods toward world market levels. The adjustment of the real exchange rate took place through inflation in Estonia's fixed exchange rate regime, while until early 1994 Latvia's policy allowed part of this adjustment to be carried out through nominal appreciation, a factor that largely explains Latvia's success relative to Estonia in inflation performance. In Lithuania, until spring 1993, price increases—instead of the exchange rate—were the chief channel for real appreciation. While possibilities for price arbitrage in the tradable goods sector surely have diminished in all three countries, it appears that the real exchange rate may still remain below its equilibrium level (see below) and inflationary pressures from this source may continue to be present for still some time, although to a lesser degree than before.

Once the price arbitrage process is over, however, prices of tradable goods should move in tandem with world market prices barring exchange rate variations, the elimination of which is presently a major goal of each Baltic central bank.[18] But inflation (abstracting from the removal of remaining subsidization) may still remain higher than in trading partner countries owing to productivity growth differentials between the tradable and nontradable goods sectors.[19] This latter point can be illustrated by regarding domestic inflation as the sum of the change in the price level of traded goods and the productivity growth differential between the traded and nontraded goods sectors. With lagging productivity growth in the nontradable goods sector and competitive wage setting, prices of home goods tend to rise faster than in the tradable goods sector where price equalization with world market prices takes place through commodity arbitrage. As a result, the overall inflation is higher than world inflation but is not necessarily inconsistent with external equilibrium.

In addition, with higher productivity growth than in its trading partners, a country would benefit from better profitability in the tradable goods sector. This, in turn, would lead to capital inflows and add to real appreciation either through inflation (fixed rate) or nominal appreciation (floating rate). However, as this real appreciation reflects a movement in the equilibrium real exchange rate, it is sustainable. The data in the Baltic countries suggest that with renewed economic growth, this kind of process may well be under way and explain why inflation has remained at current, relatively high levels. Recent production estimates suggest that output has begun to recover in all Baltic countries. Meanwhile, industrial employment has declined and new jobs are created mainly in services, that is, in the nontradable goods sector. This suggests that productivity gains in the tradable goods

---

[17]Unpaid heating bills and rents, in particular, have been common during the early stages of the reform in major cities in the Baltic countries.

[18]Variations in the real exchange rate between the Baltic currencies and the Russian ruble have occasionally contributed to the Baltic inflation. For example, the acceleration of inflation in all three Baltic countries in late 1993 largely reflected the real appreciation of the Russian ruble at that time.
[19]See Balassa (1964).

sector could be significant. Also, in particular in Estonia, strong inflows of foreign direct investment have supported productivity growth in the tradable goods sector.

Output Developments in Perspective

Stabilization of output has taken place relatively rapidly in the Baltic countries. Real GDP declined cumulatively by between 30 and 50 percent in 1991–93 compared with between 16 and 23 percent in Poland, Hungary, and the former Czechoslovakia in the similar time period of 1990–92 (Chart 1.6). However, within two years after the reform, all three Baltic countries reported that the output decline had bottomed out. In Estonia, several indicators (real GDP, industrial output, retail sales) suggest that the recovery had already begun in the first half of 1993. Recovery in Latvia is estimated to have started in late 1993, and in Lithuania in early 1994. For 1994, preliminary estimates suggest positive growth in all three countries. Despite the fact that the Baltic stabilization programs started about two years later than in Central Europe, they are estimated to have recorded similar growth rates in 1994.

Part of this rapid recovery of output can be explained by the steeper initial decline due to the more severe systemic and terms of trade shocks than in Central Europe at the outset of the reform process. There were also several supply side characteristics that could have contributed to the rapid stabilization of output. Thus, the initial allocation of labor and capital may have been less distorted in the Baltic countries than in Russia and other economies of the former Soviet Union. The labor force, with high skills and low labor costs that characterize the comparative advantage of the Baltic countries, and capital were largely concentrated in light and consumption goods industries (food processing, textile, and light metal) (Table 1.4). This initial industrial structure made it possible to shift exports from declining markets in the countries of the former Soviet Union to stable markets in industrial countries without massive reallocation of labor and capital. In addition, that the Baltic countries had been an experimental area in the Soviet planning system in these industries may have put them in a better position to take advantage of the new opportunities offered by a more market-oriented economy.

Another important factor in the rapid output stabilization was the level of labor costs. The $30 a month, or so, average wage in the Baltic countries, at the time of the adoption of the stabilization programs was low compared with about $200 in Poland, and a similar or even higher wage in Hungary and the former Czechoslovakia. While productivity differentials may explain part of these large differ-

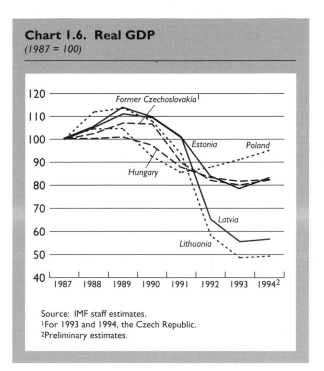

Chart 1.6. Real GDP
(1987 = 100)

Source: IMF staff estimates.
[1]For 1993 and 1994, the Czech Republic.
[2]Preliminary estimates.

ences, Baltic producers surely benefited from low initial levels of unit labor costs relative to Central Europe. The low-cost level of the Baltic countries helped them shift exports away from the markets of Russia and other former Soviet Union countries. Moreover, the high purchasing power of the neighboring Nordic countries with high labor costs provided a nearby market and effective demand for Baltic exports. And perhaps even more important, the prospect for foreign direct investment in the Baltic area became attractive since low-cost, skilled labor combined with an obsolete inherited capital stock made the expected rate of return on new direct investments high. Indeed, as regards foreign direct investment, which was also stimulated by the stabilization of the macroeconomic environment, an important difference between the Baltic countries and Central Europe was that at the time of the Baltic reforms, the political risk in investing in these countries may have been smaller than in Central Europe at the time of reforms in 1990–91 in that the Soviet Union still existed, presumably adding to the risk premium for foreign direct investments.[20]

Both trade and price liberalization were crucial for the recovery in output in the Baltic countries, as

---

[20]While the share of foreign direct investment of purchasing power GDP in Estonia was second only to Hungary in 1993, among transition economies the share in Latvia and Lithuania also exceeded that in Poland, although it was smaller than in the former Czechoslovakia. See EBRD (1994).

Table 1.4. Industrial Specialization in the Baltic Countries in 1988
(Baltic share of output for selected industrial products in the former U.S.S.R.)

	Estonia	Latvia	Lithuania
Share of total value added	0.6	1.1	1.4
Share of			
Alterating current electric motors	2.3	. . .	4.6
Metal-cutting machines	. . .	. . .	6.6
Equipment for livestock and fodder products	0.4	4.2	2.6
Excavators	4.5	. . .	. . .
Mineral fertilizers	0.6	0.5	1.8
Synthetic fibers	3.3	0.9	. . .
Paper	1.5	2.2	1.9
Cement	0.8	0.5	2.4
Roofing materials	. . .	. . .	2.4
Bricks	0.6	1.0	2.4
Window glass	0.8	1.6	1.7
Cotton cloth	2.3	0.7	1.2
Woolen cloth	1.1	2.2	3.1
Silk cloth	0.5	1.3	2.4
Hosiery	0.8	3.7	5.0
Knitted garments	1.2	2.2	3.2
Shoes	0.9	1.2	1.4
Radios	. . .	17.4	. . .
Televisions, all	. . .	. . .	6.2
Televisions, color	. . .	. . .	4.6
Tape recorders	. . .	1.7	3.3
Refrigerators	. . .	3.2	5.5
Vacuum cleaners	. . .	. . .	3.6
Electric irons	. . .	8.2	. . .
Washing machines	. . .	4.2	. . .
Bicycles, children's	. . .	4.0	2.6
Furniture	2.2	2.1	2.3
Sugar	. . .	1.9	1.8
Meat products	1.4	1.9	3.4
Fish products	3.6	4.9	3.7
Lard	1.8	2.7	4.5
Canned goods	1.7	2.4	2.0

Source: IMF, World Bank, OECD, and EBRD, *A Study of the Soviet Economy*, Vol. 1 (Paris, February 1991).

well as in Central Europe. However, as discussed above, the Baltic countries made more rapid progress in abolishing subsidies, and thus hardening the budget constraints in the enterprise sector. This may have contributed to a sharper initial decline of output in the Baltic countries, but it would also explain the more rapid recovery as enterprises became exposed to the new relative price structure determined by the world market and were forced to adjust or go out of business. Central European countries may have suffered more from attempts to halt the decline in output by providing subsidies that delayed the transition process and recovery.

The relatively strong financial discipline among Baltic enterprises has also benefited from the general avoidance of moral hazard problems in dealing with troubled banks and enterprises. Large-scale bailouts of banks and enterprises have been avoided so far, although such pressures may still arise with further restructuring of the banking system and enterprise sector. Also, bankruptcy legislation has been enforced successfully, in particular in Estonia.[21] Sim-

[21]There have been 200 to 300 bankruptcy proceedings since autumn 1992 in Estonia, compared with 1,045 in Poland since 1990 (EBRD (1994)).

ilarly, Estonia's treatment of the banking crisis in late 1992 and early 1993 stands out as an example of introducing hard budget constraints through discipline in the banking sector.[22] Although some recapitalization of the banking system took place through a government bond issue, the scheme appears stricter than in many Central European bailout schemes. For example, in Poland, the government recapitalized seven large banks by treasury bonds in 1993, and in the former Czechoslovakia, considerable sums were injected into the banking system to add to banks' capital in 1991.[23]

Did the Policy Regime Matter?

The stabilization performance of the Baltic countries has much in common with the predictions of the standard exchange rate versus money-based stabilization models.[24] These models, and experiences in other countries, would predict Estonia's fixed exchange regime to yield a rapid disinflation and better initial growth performance than in Latvia and Lithuania, which first let their exchange rate float and relied on controls of monetary aggregates as major tools of stabilization. With a credible disinflation program, the fixed exchange regime would bring down inflation rapidly. Nominal interest rates, being linked to the anchor country's interest rate levels, would decline more leading to declining real interest rates owing to remaining inflation inertia, stronger demand, and more buoyant output. However, with inflation inertia, real appreciation would emerge, and, if exceeding the equilibrium real exchange rate, would lead to a trade deficit. Eventually, output would fall and recession follow. A floating regime with a credible, tight monetary policy would also bring down inflation quickly. However, interest rates would remain higher than in the fixed exchange rate case, because of the lack of a link to the interest rate level in a low-inflation anchor country. Therefore, in the money-based stabilization, real interest rates would remain higher and output initially more depressed, with a further slowdown in inflation. Eventually, real interest rates would decline enough to stimulate demand, and output would begin to grow. Hence, stabilization based on the exchange rate would produce "boom first, recession later," while

a money-based program would introduce a pattern of "recession first, boom later." While these "stylized facts" are derived from stabilization models that emphasize demand factors as crucial forces at work, the adjustment pattern remains similar even if supply side factors are taken into account.[25] Chart 1.7 shows developments in inflation, real interest rate, real exchange rate, and real GDP in the Baltic countries, and the following discussion attempts to shed more light on these adjustment patterns.

Disinflation and Policy Credibility

Following the implementation of their stabilization programs, inflation decelerated rapidly in both Estonia (fixed rate regime) and Latvia (floating rate regime), suggesting that both stabilization programs were highly credible. Indeed, it appears that Latvia, with a floating exchange rate regime and nominal appreciation, has been able to bring down inflation to slightly lower levels than Estonia with its fixed rate regime. Both of these countries have clearly outperformed Lithuania, which also applied a floating exchange rate for most of the observation period. Broadly speaking, however, the reduction of inflation has been successful in each country regardless of the exchange rate regime.

Hence, the Baltic experience does not appear to support the commonly held hypothesis that the use of a fixed exchange rate is more successful in reducing inflation than the use of money-based stabilization policies. In this respect, one problem with international evidence is that it is not clear to what extent the correlation between the exchange rate regime and disinflation reflects causality. Does the exchange rate anchor contribute in its own right to disinflation or does the correlation reflect the fact that countries that have chosen a fixed exchange rate regime instead of a floating one happened to be those most committed to pursuing disinflation through aggressive policies? If the two countries' financial policies are equally aggressive against inflation, the outcome could be the same, and the fixed regime would have no effect in its own right.

A comparison of the tightness of monetary conditions in the Baltic countries is suggestive in this respect. When measured by the growth of base and broad money, monetary conditions have been broadly similar under Estonia's currency board and Latvia's floating regime as was suggested by Chart 1.2. In other words, the same degree of policy tightening relative to the prereform period did produce a broadly similar reduction in inflation in a country with a fixed exchange rate (Estonia) as in a country

[22]As three major Estonian banks with deposits equivalent to 40 percent of money supply turned out to be both insolvent and illiquid, they were closed down; two of them were merged, and the third one was liquidated.

[23]See Ebrill (1994) and EBRD (1994).

[24]See, for example, Rodriguez (1982), Dornbusch (1982), Fischer (1986), Kiguel and Liviatan (1992), Calvo and Végh (1990) and (1993), and Dornbusch and Werner (1994).

[25]See Roldós (1995).

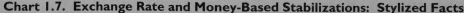

Chart 1.7. Exchange Rate and Money-Based Stabilizations: Stylized Facts

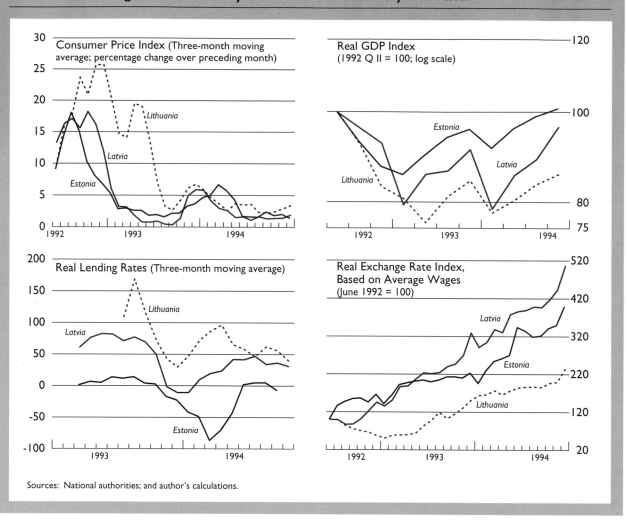

Consumer Price Index (Three-month moving average; percentage change over preceding month)

Lithuania
Latvia
Estonia

Real GDP Index
(1992 Q II = 100; log scale)

Estonia
Latvia
Lithuania

Real Lending Rates (Three-month moving average)

Lithuania
Latvia
Estonia

Real Exchange Rate Index, Based on Average Wages
(June 1992 = 100)

Latvia
Estonia
Lithuania

Sources: National authorities; and author's calculations.

with a flexible rate initially (Latvia). On the other hand, in Lithuania, both base and broad money grew faster than in Estonia and Latvia, which is consistent with Lithuania's poorer inflation performance.

As regards fiscal policy, Table 1.1 indicates that the fiscal stance, as measured by the level of the financial deficit, has remained broadly similar since mid-1992 in each country. Also, the fiscal impulse—proxied by the change in the financial balance—has been on the same order of magnitude. Hence, it does not seem that fiscal policies have been so much different that they would have produced different outcomes in inflation performance.

Thus, the evidence from the Baltic experience supports the notion that what matters for disinflation is

not so much the policy framework (e.g., fixed versus flexible exchange rate regime) but the policy content.

Interest Rates and Credibility of the Exchange Rate

It was argued above that interest rates with an exchange rate anchor would be lower than without such an anchor even if both stabilization policies were successful in reducing inflation. Indeed, interest rates, both nominal and real, appear to have remained higher in Latvia and Lithuania compared with Estonia as suggested by theory (Chart 1.8). Some observers have explained the lower interest rates in

Estonia by the supposedly greater credibility gains obtained by its currency board arrangement.[26]

There are several factors in addition to policy credibility, however, that can explain this. First, the higher lending rates in Latvia and Lithuania could partly reflect slower restructuring of the enterprise sector associated with lower creditworthiness of borrowers, and thus higher risks involved in banks' lending operations. Also, banks in Latvia and Lithuania may have been more compelled than in Estonia to push up lending rates to improve their capital ratios, given the slower restructuring in the financial market, and therefore, weaker solvency.[27] After accounting for different spreads, the lending rate differential of Latvia and Lithuania vis-à-vis Estonia of 23–32 percentage points converts into a deposit rate differential of 15–18 percentage points in October 1994 (Table 1.5). However, higher deposit rates in Latvia and Lithuania relative to Estonia could largely reflect the lower confidence of the Latvian and Lithuanian depositors in their banking systems, that is, the higher risk of bank default, which increases banks' funding costs. Abstracting from this factor and comparing the auction interest rates on nonrisk government assets (i.e., short-term certificates of deposit (CDs) of the Bank of Estonia and treasury bills in Latvia and Lithuania) indicates that rates for low-risk financial assets are indeed lower than deposit rates, suggesting about a 5–6 percentage point risk premium for bank deposits in these countries in October 1994. The remaining interest rate differentials (i.e., 15–18 percentage point) could thus reflect some residual risk differentials and different exchange rate premiums between the Baltic countries.

In principle, the interest rate differential between domestic and foreign nonrisk assets could detect the risk premium that the public sets on the exchange rate. However, a comparison of the above auction rates to detect this premium is not straightforward. Measuring parities for interest rates through results from a central bank credit auction may include an upward bias because of the adverse selection problem.[28] The auctions in Latvia and Lithuania, however, are not for central bank credit (a liability of the banks) but for treasury bills (asset). The adverse risk selection argument would not apply in this case. Nonetheless, it is still possible that some residual credit risk applies to government securities (Latvia and Lithuania) in comparison with central bank securities (Estonia),

as only the latter are guaranteed to be honored in cash (which is also a central bank liability).

Indeed, given these caveats, a comparison of domestic and foreign currency deposit rates may be more accurate in measuring the degree of the exchange rate credibility, in particular in Latvia and Lithuania. This comparison suggests a small exchange rate risk (3–4 percent) for the Estonian kroon in 1994.[29] For Latvia and Lithuania, this risk premium was much higher in early 1994 but by October 1994, it had declined to some 10 percent in Latvia and 6 percent in Lithuania for a maturity of three to six months. At that time, perhaps one half of the lending and deposit rate differentials between Lithuania and Estonia reflected exchange rate risk considerations. As for Latvia, the risk premium on the exchange rate may have explained one third of the lending rate differential relative to Estonia, and less than half of the deposit rate differential.

The above decomposition of the interest rate differentials between the Baltic countries indicates that for the most part they are likely to reflect other factors than credibility considerations.[30] The exchange rate risk premiums in Latvia and Lithuania, however, do suggest that Estonia's stabilization and lower levels of interest rates may have to some extent gained from the credibility effects associated with its currency board arrangement. Such a conclusion is also supported by the developments of interest rates in Lithuania before and after the adoption of the currency board arrangement. Measured by the differential between domestic and foreign currency deposit rates, the exchange rate risk premium declined steeply from some 40 percent in March, that is, one month before the adoption of the currency board, to only 6 percent in October, indicating a strong improvement of confidence in the Lithuanian currency. Hence, the above discussion suggests that, while credibility factors may have been indifferent as regards successful disinflation in the Baltic countries, they may have had some role to play as regards the interest rate levels and may have affected the level of economic activity in the early phase of the reform process.

There is another way to test this latter proposition. That is, to see whether inflation was brought

---

[26]See Hansson and Sachs (1994).

[27]For the stage of enterprise restructuring and financial reform in the transition economies (including the Baltic countries), see EBRD (1994).

[28]See Mathieson and Haas (1994).

[29]However, comparing Estonia's interbank market or the Bank of Estonia's CD rates to German money market rates suggests full credibility of the Estonian kroon.

[30]This conclusion is also supported by the observation (subject to qualifications due to GDP measurement problems) that the income velocity of money appears to have declined earlier in Latvia than in Estonia suggesting faster remonetization and rapid confidence buildup in the economy.

Chart 1.8. Interest Rates in the Baltic Countries
(Three-month moving average)

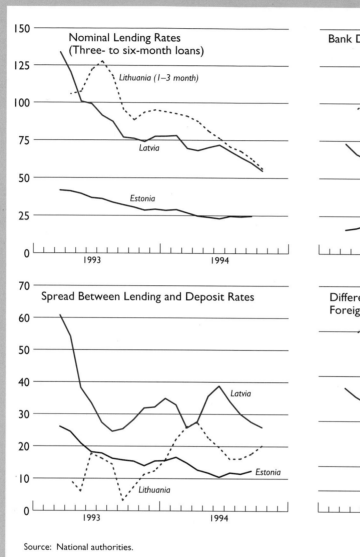

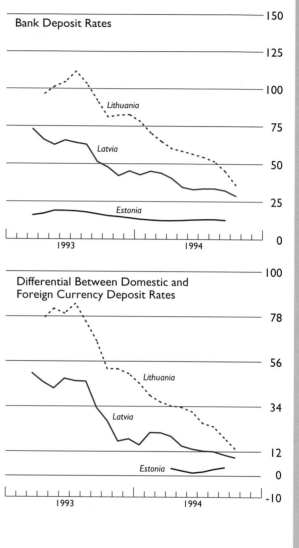

Source: National authorities.

down with smaller output cost in Estonia than in Latvia and Lithuania. The underlying argument to test is that with full credibility of the exchange rate and with flexible prices, disinflation should involve no, or only limited, output losses. Hence, with better credibility in the exchange rate and thus lower real interest rates, Estonia's disinflation process should have coincided with smaller output declines since mid-1992. Chart 1.9 indicates that Latvia's inflation has declined to the lowest level among the Baltic countries. At the same time, however, output losses

have been more pronounced than in Estonia.[31] In

---

[31]The indices of quarterly real GDP were smoothed by estimating a quadratic trend over the period 1992 Q2 to 1994 Q4. Trend estimates were based on the following equations:

$$Y_{est} = 103.2 - 4.33 * Time + 0.36 * (Time)^2$$
$$(19.3) \quad (2.5) \qquad\quad (3.0)$$

$$Y_{lat} = 114.8 - 8.27 * Time + 0.55 * (Time)^2$$
$$(16.3) \quad (3.7) \qquad\quad (3.5)$$

$$Y_{lit} = 112.6 - 8.65 * Time + 0.55 * (Time)^2$$
$$(22.2) \quad (5.3) \qquad\quad (4.8)$$

where Y denotes the real GDP, and values in brackets are t-statistics.

Table 1.5. Interest Rate Differentials Between the Baltic Countries, 1994
(In percent a year)

	Estonia		Latvia		Lithuania	
	March	October	March	October	March	October
Lending rate (3–6 months)	23.9	22.5	69.5	54.7	79.2	45.0
Differential versus Estonia	...	...	45.6	32.2	55.3	22.5
Domestic deposit rate (3–6 months)	11.6	11.2	43.8	28.8	73.0	26.5
Differential versus Estonia	...	...	32.2	17.6	61.1	15.3
Foreign exchange deposit rate (3–6 months)	7.9	7.9	22.7	18.9	33.3	20.6
Differential versus Estonia	...	...	14.8	11.0	25.4	12.7
Spread (1–2)	12.3	11.3	25.7	25.9	6.2	18.5
Auction rate[1]	5.6	5.8	23.8	23.3	...	20.9
Exchange rate risk[2]	3.7	3.3	21.1	9.9	39.7	5.9

Source: The Baltic central banks.
[1] The Bank of Estonia's certificate-of-deposit rate (28 days) for Estonia, treasury bill rates (30 days) for Latvia and Lithuania.
[2] Domestic deposit rate minus foreign exchange deposit rate.

Lithuania, inflation has been highest while output losses have been most severe.

A more specific calculation of such a sacrifice ratio is presented in Table 1.6. The results suggest that since the beginning of the stabilization programs, each 100 percentage point decline in the 12-month inflation rate has involved a loss in real GDP of only 0.7 percentage point in Estonia.[32] In Latvia, the loss of output was somewhat higher (1.7 percentage points), and it was highest in Lithuania (2.7 percentage points). These observations can be interpreted in the first place to be consistent with the earlier discussed relative levels of interest rates, which could largely reflect such structural impediments as different degrees of enterprise creditworthiness and

[32] The cumulative loss of output between 1992 Q2 and 1994 Q4 is calculated according to the following formula:

$$L = \left\{ \frac{\sum\limits_{t=1}^{10} (y^*_t - y_t)}{\sum\limits_{t=1}^{10} y^*_t} \right\} *100,$$

where L is the cumulative percentage loss of real output, Y^* is the initial level, and y the actual level of real GDP, and t denotes time subscript.

varying confidence in the financial systems. Moreover, the results of this crude test must be qualified as regards other exogenous factors affecting the output performance during the transition. For example, while the high level of foreign direct investment in Estonia relative to Latvia and Lithuania may partly reflect credibility considerations, it surely is owing also to Estonia's closer historical, political, and cultural links to Finland and Sweden, the major foreign investors in Estonia. Similarly, the test does not allow for differences in supply side disturbances; for example, Lithuania was particularly hard hit by energy shortages in 1992. Also, the speed of privatization has been different; Latvia recording the slowest progress among the Baltic countries. However, it cannot be excluded that part of the explanation also lies in different levels of policy credibility as measured by the risk premium of the exchange rate embodied in the interest rate differentials between the Baltic countries.

Real Exchange Rate

A key feature in the exchange rate based, as well as money-based stabilization process is the real appreciation of the currency. In a fixed regime the real appreciation could lead to a recession after an initial boom, while in a money-based stabilization, the real exchange rate would initially appreciate but depreciate later with stimulative effects on output. The Baltic experience is somewhat different, however, at least as regards the initial stages of stabilization. As was noted before, the currencies of the Baltic countries were highly undervalued against the currencies in industrial countries at the beginning of the reform. Apart from the general issue of overvaluation and its detrimental effects, two considerations follow from such a starting position. First, what were the benefits, if any, for the stabilization strategy? Second, to what extent does such an undervaluation pose risks for the stabilization of prices? To be sure, the real exchange rate in each country has appreciated considerably since the beginning of the reform; based on consumer prices, the real exchange rate of

Estonia's kroon against the U.S. dollar appreciated by over 200 percent between mid-1992 and end-1994, Latvia's lats and Lithuania's litas by nearly 350 percent (Chart 1.10).[33]

From the perspective of the stabilization strategy, there have been several advantages for the Baltic countries from this initial undervaluation, gradual appreciation approach. First, it has served well in making their products competitive in Western markets and reorienting exports away from Russia and other countries of the former Soviet Union. This, in turn, has spurred the importation and development of capital, new technologies, skills, and thus productivity. Second, a sharp increase in dollar wages has improved the purchasing power of the population in terms of imported goods, which now comprise about one half of goods consumed. Realizing these benefits has been important in mobilizing popular support for the reforms. Third, to the extent that the real appreciation has resulted from nominal strengthening of the currency (e.g., in Latvia), it has helped keep inflation in check. On the negative side, as mentioned before, initial undervaluation of the currency together with a fixed exchange rate may work against bringing down inflation. This can gradually weaken a country's competitiveness and thus, in an open economy, its foundation for growth. The Baltic experience, however, suggests that these latter considerations may not be too important in the early stages of stabilization for several reasons.

First, the inflationary bias originating from setting the exchange rate at an undervalued level, either intentionally or in the absence of firm knowledge about the equilibrium level of the real exchange rate, may not be too important in circumstances where a country's past inflation has been as high as 15–20 percent a month. What matters initially is to reverse such a path toward hyperinflation and move to a regime of significantly reduced inflation. Fixing the nominal rate at existing "market" levels (even if this rate is considered undervalued), combined with sound financial policies, provided an anchor for such a reduction of inflation in Estonia, even though price arbitrage continued owing to the exchange rate disequilibrium. Estonia's monthly inflation was halved from 14 percent in the period April–August 1992 to 7 percent in the period September–December 1992, to 2¼ percent during the first half of 1993, and to below 2 percent in the second half of 1994. In this case, the initial undervaluation of the exchange rate did not turn around the disinflation process. To further illustrate the magnitudes

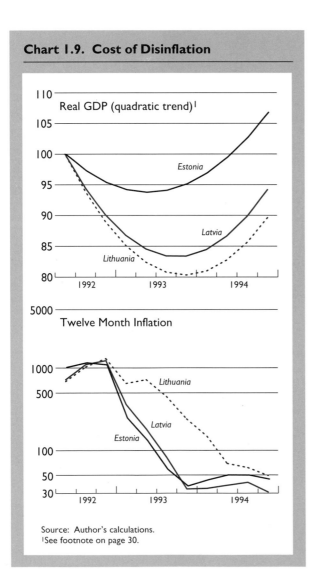

Chart I.9. Cost of Disinflation

Real GDP (quadratic trend)[1]

Estonia

Latvia

Lithuania

1992   1993   1994

Twelve Month Inflation

Lithuania

Latvia

Estonia

1992   1993   1994

Source: Author's calculations.
[1]See footnote on page 30.

---

[33]However, if the real exchange rate is computed based on wage inflation, which may be a more appropriate indicator of the external competitiveness, the real appreciation remains smaller in Lithuania than in Estonia and Latvia.

Table 1.6. Disinflation and Output Loss

	Estonia	Latvia	Lithuania		Estonia	Latvia	Lithuania
	(Real GDP index)				(Twelve-month inflation)		
1992							
QII	100.0	100.0	100.0		1,029	723	688
QIII	93.0	96.3	92.5		1,167	1,100	1,031
QIV	87.0	92.7	83.2		1,102	1,222	1,294
1993							
QI	85.7	79.6	80.9		253	363	652
QII	90.0	85.8	76.2		134	182	723
QIII	94.0	86.6	81.3		60	83	452
QIV	95.9	91.3	84.5		37	34	241
1994							
QI	91.5	78.8	78.1		44	34	148
QII	96.0	85.6	80.5		51	38	69
QIII	98.9	89.1	83.8		51	41	62
QIV	100.9	96.5	85.8		45	31	49
Output loss							
In percent (−)							
End of period	0.9	−3.5	−14.2				
Cumulative[1]	−6.7	−11.8	−17.3				
Disinflation							
(in percentage point)			Since 1992 QII		984	692	639
Cumulative output loss in percent							
(per 100 units of disinflation)			Since 1992 QII		−0.7	−1.7	−2.7

Source: Author's calculations.
[1]See footnote 32 on page 17.

involved: when Lithuania adopted its currency board, there was some debate about the appropriate level of the exchange rate. However, setting the U.S. dollar rate of the litas at 3.8 or 4.2, the levels at which opposing views existed, represented a difference of only some 10 percent—an increase in the price level that would in any event have taken place in about two months in the inflation environment immediately preceding the pegging. The lower the immediate past inflation, however, the more important it is to find a "correct" initial level of the fixed exchange rate.

Second, as regards competitiveness, the initial undervaluation leaves room for real appreciation without undermining export performance, and thereby can be an important factor for economic recovery. If a country simultaneously gains in productivity relative to trade partners, the level of the equilibrium real exchange rate would rise, thus leaving further room for real appreciation. Such a catch-up effect may result from trade liberalization, low wage costs, and an upgrading in the capital

stock (in part due to foreign direct investment) leading to high marginal productivity of capital. In this case, overall inflation in a transition country may for some time exceed that in its main trading partners without threatening the sustainability of a fixed exchange rate (or managed floating) regime. Hence, the Baltic experience suggests that the key to success is to ensure that the initial exchange rate is not overvalued, or excessively undervalued; otherwise, the precise level may not be too important.

While it is difficult to establish the equilibrium level of the real exchange rate to which the Baltic currencies would converge, some light on this issue can be shed by analyzing current developments in the trade balance, export performance, foreign direct investment and foreign reserves, and interest rate differentials. In light of these indirect indicators of competitiveness, it can be argued that so far (by the end of 1994) the Baltic real exchange rates have not been at excessive levels.

As shown in Chart 1.11, there was a deterioration in the trade balance in Estonia since the end of

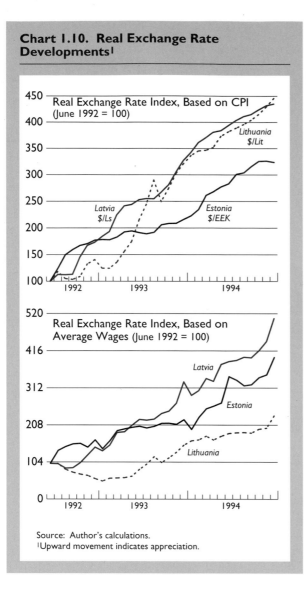

Chart 1.10. Real Exchange Rate Developments[1]

Real Exchange Rate Index, Based on CPI
(June 1992 = 100)

Lithuania $/Lit

Latvia $/Ls

Estonia $/EEK

1992   1993   1994

Real Exchange Rate Index, Based on Average Wages (June 1992 = 100)

Latvia

Estonia

Lithuania

1992   1993   1994

Source: Author's calculations.
[1]Upward movement indicates appreciation.

upgrading the Latvian telecommunication system. Interest rate differentials between domestic and foreign assets may be related to doubts about the sustainability of the recent real appreciation, but these differentials have been declining since early 1994. In Lithuania, the trade deficit declined during 1993 and was relatively stable in 1994. At the same time, Lithuania's dollar exports continued to increase although foreign direct investments were picking up only slowly. Foreign reserves have increased rapidly, in particular since the introduction of the currency board; and interest rate differentials diminished substantially.

If competitiveness is to be maintained, however, continued real appreciation either through higher-than-abroad inflation or nominal appreciation requires a good degree of real wage flexibility to maintain profitability in the tradable goods sector. Based on the rapid response of the Baltic real wages to adverse external shocks in 1991–92, it would appear that this flexibility has been high, at least so far. However, caution in conclusions is warranted, as it appears that under the conditions of high inflation, wage and price rigidities generally tend to be small as experienced in several countries of the former Soviet Union. The decline of real wages after the price shocks in early 1992 can well be explained by the remaining legacy of a planning economy, as prices were partially liberalized but wages were still used as a nominal anchor, preventing wage response to higher prices and leading to a real wage decline.[34]

Nevertheless, in an environment of free price and wage setting, the Baltic labor market could remain quite flexible if current institutional patterns are maintained. In the absence of strong trade unions there has not been room for Western European-type, insider-outsider phenomena. Also, unemployment compensation and related social benefits have remained at levels that do not distort incentives for job search, skill enhancement, and occupational mobility. In addition, the role of the minimum wage as a leading indicator for higher reservation wages and budgetary social expenditures has eroded with declines in the replacement ratios and dismantling or weakening of the links between the minimum wage and social benefits. Finally, the Baltic governments have so far been successful in resisting demands for various wage and price indexation schemes.

Conclusion

The Baltic countries have made significant progress in macroeconomic stabilization. Their experience highlights several factors, partly general and partly

1992, and since mid-1993 in Latvia, raising a question of possible overvaluation of the exchange rate. Estonia's exports, however, have continued to increase at very rapid rates in U.S. dollar terms; foreign direct investment was very buoyant; and foreign reserves continued to increase; all suggesting confidence in the currency. In addition, as was noted above, the interest rate differential of non-risk, short-term securities between Estonia and Germany, the anchor currency for the Estonian kroon, remained small.

In Latvia, dollar exports also remained on a rising trend, and foreign reserves increased rapidly. Foreign direct investments, although still at a much lower level than in Estonia, have begun to rise, reflecting, inter alia, strong foreign participation in

---

[34]See Sahay and Végh (1995).

Chart 1.11. Indirect Indicators of Competitiveness

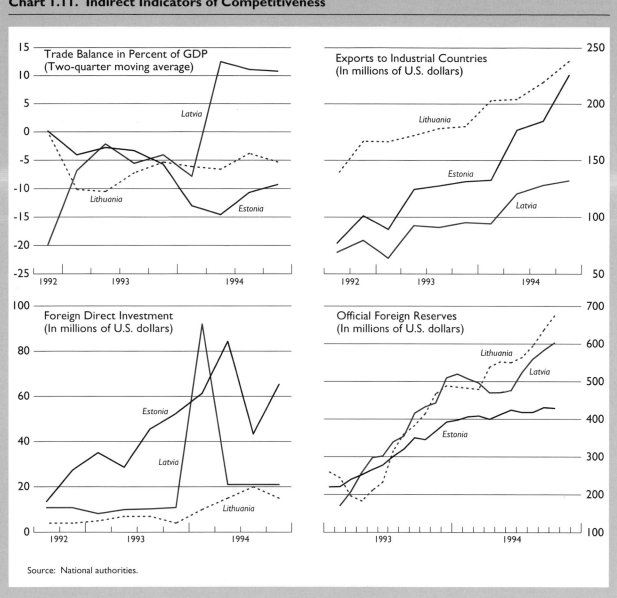

Source: National authorities.

specific, which have made their transition process successful so far. In fact, during the first two-to-three years into serious reform, inflation has fallen more than, for example, in Poland during a corresponding period after the "big bang." Within the same period, the output cost of this disinflation process has remained small in Estonia and rather limited in Latvia and Lithuania. There is little doubt that one of the key explanations for this has been the Baltic authorities' apparent and early determination to take rapid action to liberalize the economy and adopt

strong stabilization policies, an attitude enhanced by the political events in the late 1980s and early 1990s before they regained their independence.

There have been several specific factors that help explain the Baltic success in stabilization. Strong commitment to sound financial policies has been absolutely crucial. Solid fiscal positions throughout 1992–94 helped establish the credibility of strong monetary policies, particularly in Estonia and Latvia, and more recently also in Lithuania. Similarly, it appears that the credibility of these policies has been of greater importance than the choice of the exchange rate regime per se. In light of the Baltic experience, the choice of such a regime may not make significant difference in terms of bringing down inflation. To some extent, it may be reflected in the timing of the output variations, although the evidence for such causality remains weak given the large number of exogenous factors affecting output developments during the transition. The appreciation of the real exchange rate in each country, which has continued since the outset of the reform, has thus far been sustainable, and there are signs that the recovery of output that is taking place in each country is also sustainable.

References

Balassa, Bela, "The Purchasing Power Parity: A Reappraisal," *Journal of Political Economy* (December 1964).

Bennett, Adam, "The Operation of the Estonian Currency Board," *Staff Papers*, International Monetary Fund, Vol. 40 (June 1993), pp. 451–70.

———, "Currency Boards: Issues and Experiences," IMF Paper on Policy Analysis and Assessment, PPAA/94/18 (Washington: International Monetary Fund, September 1994).

Calvo, Guillermo A., and Carlos A. Végh, "Credibility and the Dynamics of Stabilization Policy: A Basic Framework," IMF Working Paper, WP/90/110 (Washington: International Monetary Fund, November 1990).

———, "Inflation Stabilization and Nominal Anchors," IMF Paper on Policy Analysis and Assessment, PPAA/92/4 (Washington: International Monetary Fund, December 1992).

———, "Stabilization Dynamics and Backward-Looking Contracts," IMF Working Paper, WP/93/29 (Washington: International Monetary Fund, March 1993).

Dornbusch, Rudiger, "Stabilization Policies in Developing Countries: What Have We Learned?" *World Development*, Vol. 10, No. 9 (1982), pp. 701–708.

———, and Alejandro Werner, "Mexico: Stabilization, Reform, and No Growth," Brookings Papers on Economic Activity 1/1994 (Washington: Brookings Institution, 1994).

Ebrill, Liam P., and others, *Poland: The Path to a Market Economy*, IMF Occasional Paper, No. 113 (Washington: International Monetary Fund, October 1994).

European Bank for Reconstruction and Development (EBRD), *Transition Report* (London: EBRD, October 1994).

Fischer, Stanley, "Indexing, Inflation, and Economic Policy" (Cambridge, Massachusetts: MIT Press, 1986).

Hansson, Ardo, and Jeffrey Sachs, "Monetary Institutions and Credible Stabilization: A Comparison of Experiences in the Baltics," paper presented at a conference on Central Banks in Eastern Europe and the Newly Independent States, University of Chicago Law School, April 22–23, 1994.

International Monetary Fund, *Lithuania*, IMF Economic Reviews, No. 6 (Washington: IMF, August 1994).

Kiguel, Miguel A., and Nissan Liviatan, "The Business Cycle Associated with Exchange Rate-Based Stabilizations," *The World Bank Economic Review*, Vol. 6 (1992), pp. 279–305.

Mathieson, Donald J., and Richard D. Haas, "Establishing Monetary Control in Financial Systems with Insolvent Institutions," IMF Paper on Policy Analysis and Assessment, PPAA/94/10 (Washington: International Monetary Fund, June 1994).

Rodriguez, C. A., "The Argentine Stabilization Plan of December 20th," *World Development*, Vol. 10 (1982).

Rodrik, Dani, "Making Sense of the Soviet Trade Shock in Eastern Europe: A Framework and Some Estimates," Centre for Economic Policy Research, Discussion Paper Series, No. 705 (London: CEPR, July 1992).

Roldós, Jorge E., "Supply-Side Effects of Disinflation Programs," *Staff Papers*, International Monetary Fund, Vol. 42 (March 1995), pp. 158–82.

Rostowski, Jacek, "Interenterprise Arrears in Post-Communist Economies," IMF Working Paper, WP/94/43 (Washington: International Monetary Fund, April 1994).

Sahay, Ratna, and Carlos A. Végh, "Inflation and Stabilization in Transition Economies: A Comparison with Market Economies," IMF Working Paper, WP/95/8 (Washington: International Monetary Fund, January 1995).

Tarr, David, "How Moving to World Prices Affects the Terms of Trade in 15 Countries of the Former Soviet Union," Working Papers, WPS 1074 (Washington: The World Bank January 1993).

II The Transformation Path in the Czech Republic

Biswajit Banerjee

It is a common perception that among Central and East European countries the Czech Republic has been most successful to date in moving to a market-oriented economy. Macroeconomic developments, especially as regards financial stabilization, overwhelmingly support this view. Inflation has been reduced sharply and is close to single-digit levels. Economic recovery is well under way. A robust balance of payments has made it possible to build up substantial foreign exchange reserves. A strong external position has not only overcome the need for balance of payments assistance, but has enabled the Government also to repay early the entire amount it owed to the International Monetary Fund.

The experience of the Czech Republic also stands out among transition economies in a number of other important aspects. The unemployment rate is the lowest in the region and also below that in many countries in Western Europe. The fiscal strains arising from the transformation program have been contained, and the government budget was in surplus in 1993 and 1994. The privatization program is virtually drawing to a close, and, with the completion of the second wave of privatization, about 80 percent of the assets in the economy are in private hands. The credit rating of the Czech Republic in the international capital market has been progressively upgraded and is much higher than that of any other transition economy.[1] The Government has been remarkably successful in building and maintaining proreform consensus among the population.

These achievements are noteworthy because the transition to a market economy posed considerable challenges and because the Czech Republic had to cope with the uncertainties and disruptions associated with the dissolution of the former Czech and Slovak Federal Republic (CSFR). From a structural perspective, the former CSFR was much less prepared for reform than several other planned economies in Central and Eastern Europe: the state dominated production; market mechanisms were

virtually absent; and trade was heavily oriented toward members of the former Council of Mutual Economic Assistance (CMEA). At the same time that the reform program was being launched, the external environment was deteriorating sharply, as trade with CMEA members shifted to world prices and convertible currencies and economic adjustments or crises in other CMEA countries sharply contracted the CSFR's traditional export markets. The collapse of the CMEA and the contraction of major export markets presented the former CSFR with a need for a substantial stabilization effort. A stabilization effort was also needed to prevent changes in relative prices, once prices were liberalized, from fueling inflation.

The former CSFR achieved early success in weathering the cumulated effects of a large-scale liberalization and a severe terms of trade shock that was associated with the dismantling of the CMEA trade and payments arrangements. Of course, favorable starting macroeconomic conditions—low inflation, limited monetary overhang, and a small external debt burden (as percent of GDP)—contributed to the early success. But more important to the success was a vigorous pursuit of stabilization policies comprising a pegged exchange rate and restrictive fiscal, monetary, and incomes policies.[2] The progress achieved in

---

[1]The Czech Republic is rated BAA3 by Moody's and BBB-plus by Standard & Poor's. Both of these ratings have investment grade status and are just one step below an A rating.

[2]The principal features of the reform program of 1991 are discussed in detail in Aghevli, Borensztein, and van der Willigen (1992). Also, see Dyba and Svejnar (1994). The reform program was of the "big bang" type. It included a number of structural measures—almost complete liberalization of prices and the exchange and trade systems, and preparation for a rapid privatization program—supported by a mutually reinforcing package of financial policies. Portes (1994) has argued that there was overemphasis on macroeconomic policy in the reform package, and that the former CSFR did not need to stabilize or would not have done if it had not devalued the koruna excessively. (In the months preceding the introduction of the reform measures, the external value of the koruna had been cut by nearly one half through several rounds of devaluation.) The impact of the main reform measures and the external shocks were, however, very uncertain and difficult to estimate ex ante. Further, as Šujan and Šujanova (1994) note, senior Czech officials believe that for the sake of macroeconomic stability and to limit the costs of the transformation, it was desirable to create the two initial cushions of a depreciated exchange rate and a cut in real wages.

domestic and external stabilization came under serious threat of being undermined in the second half of 1992 and early 1993 from the uncertainties associated with the dissolution of the CSFR on January 1, 1993 and the early termination of the Czech and Slovak monetary union in February 1993. Through continuing commitment to strong stabilization policies, however, the Czech Government was able to quickly overcome the shock of political and monetary separation and to regain the confidence of the international financial markets.

This paper highlights the salient achievements in financial stabilization and the progress of structural reforms in the Czech Republic and discusses the tasks that still need to be addressed. Economic transformation is far from over. A major task is to press ahead with the restructuring of enterprises. At the same time, the authorities face new challenges in safeguarding the gains of stabilization, especially with growing capital inflows fueling monetary expansion and posing a dilemma to monetary management.

Rebuilding the External Sector

The progressive improvement in the external reserves position, especially since the termination of the monetary union with Slovakia, has been impressive by any standard. Gross official reserves at the end of December 1994 stood at $6.2 billion (about four months of imports of goods and services), compared with a low of $500 million (about $1^{1}/_{2}$ weeks of imports) in February 1993. The rapid rebuilding of external balance reflects strong export performance, growing receipts from tourism, and large inflows of foreign capital.

Reorientation of Exports to Western Markets

Exports to former CMEA members fell precipitously in 1991 with the dismantling of the traditional trade and payments arrangements. But, after a sluggish start, spectacular strides have been made in reorienting exports to Western markets. The share of the European Union (EU) countries in Czech exports has jumped from 31 percent in 1990 to about 54 percent in 1994, with Germany alone accounting for one third of total exports.[3] The greater access afforded by the Association Agreement with the EU in March 1992 and a trade agreement with the

European Free Trade Association (EFTA) were both instrumental in helping to direct exports away from the former CMEA toward industrial countries. Exports to Western markets continued to grow strongly in 1993, despite depressed demand conditions in major export markets, and in 1994. At the same time, the Czech Republic has been successful in making inroads into new markets and redirecting certain items adversely affected by EU restrictions (e.g., on selected iron and steel products).[4] These gains have more than offset the steep decline in exports to Slovakia.

There is no reason to believe that the strong export performance resulted from enterprises selling their products at below-market prices to maintain their cash flow; the terms of trade improved in both 1993 and 1994. The initial depreciation of the exchange rate at the outset of the liberalization program created a substantial competitive cushion for Czech enterprises and helped reorient Czech trade. Although competitiveness has been steadily eroding, a cushion still remains relative to the pretransition period. This is apparent from the developments in unit labor costs in the Czech Republic relative to major trading partners, adjusted for relative producer price inflation—a rough indicator of the profitability of tradables relative to trade partners (Chart 2.1).

Studies on the scope for reorienting trade to Western markets (mostly based on the gravity model commonly used to predict trade flows) conclude that the scope for reorientation is much greater for the Czech Republic, given its larger initial dependence on CMEA markets, than for neighboring transition economies.[5] Also, the commodity structure of Czech exports appears to be better suited to exploiting the increased access to the EU market than those of its neighboring transition economies. Compared with Hungary and Poland, the share of agricultural products and mineral fuels (notably, coal) in Czech exports is small. With the exception of steel, and perhaps some chemical products, access to EU markets for industrial products is largely unrestricted, while markets for agricultural products and coal are struggling with overcapacity and strict regulations. The Czech Republic also has benefited from new marketing links associated with direct foreign investment, which has led to diversification of its exports. Initially, the surge in Czech exports was confined mainly to intermediate manufactured products, but since 1993 machinery and transport equipment—most of the foreign direct investment in 1991 went into this sector—and miscellaneous manufactured articles have led the growth in exports.

---

[3]The Czech Statistical Office includes the former German Democratic Republic under Germany and the EU in pre-unification and postunification years. The total export base used to derive the trade shares excludes transactions with Slovakia.

[4]Notable new markets in 1993 included China, which absorbed 10 percent of the increase in exports.

[5]See Baldwin (1994).

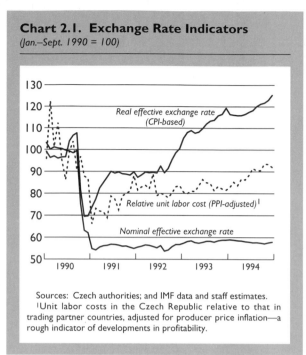

Chart 2.1. Exchange Rate Indicators
(Jan.–Sept. 1990 = 100)

Sources: Czech authorities; and IMF data and staff estimates.
¹Unit labor costs in the Czech Republic relative to that in trading partner countries, adjusted for producer price inflation—a rough indicator of developments in profitability.

Foreign Capital Inflows

Except for a brief period in late 1992 and early 1993, foreign medium- and long-term capital inflows have grown steadily. Net capital inflows amounted to the equivalent of about 12 percent of GDP in 1994, compared with 5 percent of GDP in the former CSFR in 1991. The nature of these inflows has changed markedly over the past three years. In 1991, the first year of financial stabilization, capital inflows were largely in the form of official balance of payments support from multilateral organizations and foreign bond issues by the central bank. By 1992, as the success of stabilization efforts became apparent and with the start of the privatization process, foreign private sector confidence in the Czech Republic soared; this was reflected in a surge in direct foreign investment. From 1991 to 1992, net foreign direct investment almost doubled to $1 billion. Subsequently, however, direct investment slowed as the focus of the privatization program shifted from direct sales to the distribution of vouchers, and also perhaps on account of weaker activity levels in Western Europe. The slowdown, however, has been more than offset by rapidly rising external borrowing by Czech enterprises: net borrowing rose from $340 million in 1992 to $841 million in 1993, and reached $1.4 billion in 1994. External borrowing by enterprises constituted nearly 40 percent of net capital inflows in 1994, while foreign direct investment and portfolio investment each accounted for about one fourth of the total. Since mid-1994, local governments and domestic commercial banks also have turned to raising money in international capital markets.[6]

To an extent, external borrowing by Czech enterprises has been influenced by the ex ante cost differential (including the cost of guarantees) between domestic loans and foreign loans,[7] but the main factor responsible appears to be the limited availability of long-term credit from domestic banks. The bulk of the borrowing is long term, with maturities of more than five years. No single purpose dominates borrowing; fixed investment, acquisition of real estate, and operating costs account for around one third of total borrowing. With confidence of foreign lenders in the Czech economy growing, enterprises increasingly have been able to borrow without domestic bank guarantees. In 1993, nearly 50 percent of the foreign borrowing was guaranteed by domestic banks, but this share fell to 20 percent in 1994.

Taming Inflation

After an unexpectedly large jump of about 40 percent in the first quarter of 1991, inflation declined rapidly to less than 1 percent a month by July and remained stable until August 1992. Price increases accelerated in the last four months of 1992 and culminated in a jump of the monthly rate of inflation to 8½ percent in January 1993, following the introduction of the value-added tax (VAT). Thereafter, consumer price inflation came down rapidly and was contained at 18 percent for the 12-month period ended December 1993. Excluding the contribution of the VAT and adjustments in administered prices—estimated to be 7 percentage points and 2 percentage points, respectively—price increases in 1993 were about the same as in the previous year. There was virtually no improvement in the underlying rate of inflation in 1994; inflation for the 12-month period ended December 1994 was close to 10 percent (Table 2.1).

The swift harnessing of the two price jumps was important for preventing the fueling of inflationary expectations and was achieved through tight financial policies. The underlying rate of inflation has tended to remain sticky, mainly on account of the substantial number of relative price changes that are still taking place as part of the transformation

---

[6]In May 1994, the city of Prague raised $250 million through foreign bond issues. Three large Czech banks, Komercni Banka, Investicni Banka, and Československá Obchodní Banka, have obtained syndicated loans with margins of less than 100 basis points above the London interbank offered rate (LIBOR).

[7]Taking into account the annual cost of domestic bank guarantees, typically 2–4 percent, the interest differential between domestic and foreign loans is about 2–3 percentage points.

Table 2.1. Selected Indicators

	1990	1991	1992	1993	1994 Prelim.
			(Percent change)		
Real GDP	−1.2	−14.2	−6.4	−0.9	2.6
Industrial output					
Total	−3.6	−21.6	−7.9	−5.3	2.3
Enterprises with 25 or					
more workers[1]	−3.6	−24.4	−13.8	−7.4	—
Consumer prices					
Period average	9.6	56.5	11.1	20.8	10.0
End period	15.2	52.0	12.7	18.2	10.2
Nominal wages, period average	3.7	15.4	22.5	25.2	18.5
Employment, period average	−1.0	−5.5	−1.4	−2.8	1.1
Unemployment rate					
(percent of labor force,					
end of period)	0.7	4.1	2.6	3.5	3.2
			(In billions of U.S. dollars)		
Balance of payments[2]					
Merchandise exports	9.0	7.9	8.8	10.2	11.7
Merchandise imports	9.8	7.1	10.4	11.1	12.8
Current account	−0.6	1.7	−0.1	0.1	0.1
Gross official reserves					
(end of period)	0.3	0.9	0.8	3.9	6.2
External debt in convertible					
currencies *(end of period)*	5.9	6.7	6.9	8.5	10.7
General government balance[3]					
(in percent of GDP)	0.1	−2.0	−3.6	1.4	0.5
GDP in nominal terms					
(In billions of koruna)	567	717	791	911	1,038
(In billions of U.S. dollars)	31.6	24.3	28.0	31.2	36.0

Sources: The Czech authorities; and IMF staff estimates.

[1]In 1990–91, enterprises with 100 or more employees.

[2]Includes transactions in both convertible and nonconvertible currencies, but excludes transactions with the Slovak Republic. Transactions in nonconvertible currencies converted at prevailing cross-exchange rates.

[3]Figures for 1990–92 are for the former CSFR. In 1993-94, includes privatization revenues provided to the Government by the National Property Fund to finance budgetary and quasi-budgetary operations.

process.[8] Future progress on reducing inflation is likely to be gradual because important structural rigidities remain in both goods and factor markets. These rigidities persist in part because house rents and tariffs of public utilities still remain subject to price regulation and are substantially below market prices. Rents on public housing are typically one fourth of those on private housing, which too are subject to regulation. It is estimated that full liberalization of energy prices will involve further increases of 45–50 percent for natural gas, 80–85 percent for electricity, and 15–100 percent for central heating, depending on the sort of fuel used by households. The Government's intention currently is to liberalize gradually these remaining regulated prices over the remainder of the decade.

Output and Employment Performance

Following the introduction of reforms and on account of the external shocks, output suffered.[9] The decline in economic activity was concentrated

---

[8]For example, the increase in food prices (particularly of meat) in 1994 has been mainly for supply-side reasons, as farmers continue to adjust their production levels following the elimination of subsidies and rises in costs of inputs.

[9]Factors contributing to the decline in output are discussed in Aghevli, Borensztein and van der Willigen (1992), Borensztein, Demekas, and Ostry (1992), and Čapek (1993).

mostly in 1991. Thereafter, for the next two years, real GDP fluctuated around the low level reached in the last quarter of 1991 (Chart 2.2). Economic activity had begun to rebound in the second half of 1992, but the process was interrupted in 1993 by the uncertainties associated with the dissolution of the Czech and Slovak federation and a sharp slowdown in Czech-Slovak trade. In the absence of any further exogenous shocks, a broad-based economic recovery has been under way since early 1994. After suffering a cumulative decline of about 20 percent during 1991–93, measured real GDP is estimated to have increased by 2.6 percent in 1994.[10]

The trend in output is dominated by industry, which accounts for about 35 percent of GDP. In 1991, all branches of industry experienced a pronounced decline in output, reflecting the relatively dominant impact of economy-wide factors. The pace of output decline during 1992–93 varied considerably across sectors, suggesting that sector-specific factors may have become increasingly important. In late 1993, the output decline in industry bottomed out in virtually all sectors. In cases where the recovery in 1994 was modest (e.g., textiles, and machinery and equipment), average annual output showed a further small decline because of carryover effects.

The decline in employment was far less pronounced, however, than the decline in economic activity. During 1991–93, the cumulative fall in employment was only 9 percent. The proliferation of small-scale activity in industry and construction—a result of both new entries and the breakup of existing firms—and rapid growth in the trade and services sectors provided a safety cushion against employment losses.[11] Notwithstanding the changing pattern of labor deployment, the overall picture is one of slow economic restructuring, especially in industry. Large industrial enterprises (i.e., those employing 25 or more workers) held back on labor retrenchment and were more inclined to cut work hours than the work force in the first year of the reform.[12] This is not surprising, given the uncertainties surrounding the

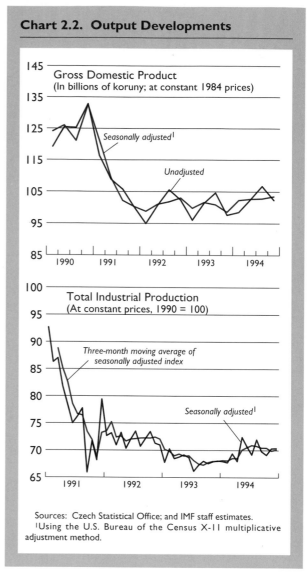

Chart 2.2. Output Developments

Sources: Czech Statistical Office; and IMF staff estimates.
[1]Using the U.S. Bureau of the Census X-11 multiplicative adjustment method.

---

[10]Compared with Poland, the Czech Republic's decline in activity was marginally higher—perhaps reflecting its greater reliance on CMEA markets—and the onset of recovery took one year longer. This delay in the recovery can be attributed to the impact of the dissolution of the Czech and Slovak federation.

[11]During 1991–93, employment in construction rose cumulatively by 12.5 percent, although output in real terms in this sector in 1993 was below its prereform level, and that in trade, restaurants, and hotels increased by about 17 percent.

[12]In 1991, employment in industrial enterprises with 25 or more workers declined by only half as much as output. Based on various measures of labor productivity, Ham, Svejnar, and Terrell (1994) have noted that hours worked in the economy declined much more steeply than employment during 1990 and 1991, but less so in 1992. A recent OECD (1994a) study also notes that most firms reacted by reducing the number of hours worked.

reform process, as enterprises may have perceived that the output decline was temporary. In addition, the pressure for downsizing was small, as incomes policy contributed to a sharp decline in product unit labor costs. There was no catch-up in labor shedding in 1992–93, with output and employment declining in parallel. However, employment in industry has continued to decline in 1994, albeit slowly, despite a turnaround in output, suggesting that the behavior of enterprises is getting increasingly market oriented. The reductions in employment in industry have taken place with few closures or bankruptcies.[13]

---

[13]Since the passage of the bankruptcy law in April 1993, only about 500 bankruptcies have taken place through the end of 1994; most of these were small companies and small entrepreneurs.

A significant feature of the Czech transformation process is that the decline in employment has not been matched by rising unemployment. After peaking at 4.4 percent in early 1992, the unemployment rate declined in the following 12 months and fluctuated between 2¹/₂ percent and 3¹/₂ percent during 1993–94. It is very likely that many of those who lost their jobs took up employment in the significantly underrecorded services sector, especially in tourism-related activities that have been booming since the introduction of reform. An additional escape valve has been employment opportunities in neighboring Germany and Austria.[14] But, by far the most important factor that kept unemployment down, especially in 1991, has been the withdrawal of a large number of workers of pensionable age from the labor force. The number of working pensioners, who accounted for about one tenth of the economically active population in 1990, contracted by over 40 percent in 1991, and the fall continued in the succeeding years, though at a much slower pace. The shift was to a large extent policy induced. Specifically, with a view to facilitating the employment of younger workers, the Government doubled the payroll tax applied to pension age workers at the start of 1991.[15]

The Government's "active" employment policies have also served to keep unemployment down, especially since 1992. Since mid-1991, the Czech Republic has had in place special programs to promote employment, the most important of which provide grants and subsidies for long-term jobs, short-term public works type jobs, retraining schemes, and employment subsidies for high school and college graduates. In 1992, the number of persons removed from the unemployment register and placed in various active employment schemes exceeded 125,000 (equivalent to more than half of the total number of unemployed). The scope of active employment policies was narrowed in 1993, as the policymakers felt that the risk of mass unemployment had receded.

Restructuring and Privatization

The slow response of enterprise restructuring to the introduction of market forces and prices can be attributed to a large extent to the Government's transformation strategy: a program of rapid privatization and leaving the task of restructuring to the private owners. Although the Czech Republic has adopted the fastest possible privatization mechanism, a certain amount of lead time is unavoidable for privatizing state enterprises, given the massive scale and coverage of the operation. During the intervening period, until new managers assume control, it is not surprising if existing managers postpone investment decisions and fundamental organizational changes.

The legal framework for enforcing financial discipline and encouraging enterprise restructuring was put in place only in April 1993. The delay in introducing the bankruptcy law was prompted by the Government's desire to prevent bankruptcies from interfering with the privatization process itself. As the privatization program was then still ongoing, the law explicitly protects enterprises from bankruptcy proceedings until the transfer of property to new owners. This is a major reason for the relatively small number of bankruptcies thus far. Tüma (1994) notes an additional reason: in some instances, when an enterprise is large and its closure would lead to an intolerable level of regional unemployment or wipe out the windfall wealth of a large interest group, the Government has been reluctant to see bankruptcy proceedings being initiated by the major creditors and has come to the rescue of the enterprise.[16] Yet another reason is that banks have not been eager to initiate bankruptcy proceedings themselves because of insufficient loan-loss provisioning for the bad loans in their portfolios.

Privatization of small enterprises was completed in 1992. Privatization of large enterprises has been implemented in two waves and has involved conventional sales to domestic and foreign investors as well as transfers of shares in enterprises to citizens through a voucher scheme. In both waves, the voucher scheme accounted for about one third of the book value of total assets privatized. The first wave was concluded in May 1993.[17] The second wave effectively came to an end at mid-November 1994 with the completion of the last round of bidding in the

---

[14]Starting from a small base in 1989, the German authorities estimate that there are now close to 50,000 Czechs legally employed in Germany, most of whom commute daily across the border into Bavaria under a special arrangement.

[15]Although a court ruling forced a repeal of the measure in late 1992, the restructuring in the age profile of the employed was an accomplished fact by then. A recent OECD (1994b) study notes that the labor participation rate of women has also fallen significantly since the introduction of reforms. This has been influenced by the difficult re-employment prospects for women out of work and by rising costs for child-care facilities combined with a persistent lack of part-time jobs.

[16]Measures taken by the Government in this regard have typically been in the form of credit guarantees by the National Property Fund, participation in debt-equity swaps by the Consolidation Bank, and other forms of financial and restructuring arrangements with the major creditors.

[17]For details of the Czech privatization program, see Ministry for the Administration of National Property and its Privatization (1993), *PlanEcon Report* (1992), and Shafik (1993).

voucher scheme; the shares were distributed to voucher holders in February 1995. With this, an estimated 80 percent of assets in the economy are in private hands.

With new owners of the privatized enterprises expected to play the main role in restructuring and strengthening corporate governance, Investment Privatization Funds (IPFs) have a key role. They hold about 65–70 percent of the shares privatized through the voucher mechanism. Following the completion of the first wave of large-scale privatization, the IPFs have been active in evaluating the situation of enterprises in their portfolios. A priority has been to initiate organizational changes and new marketing arrangements—areas in which the IPFs have ready expertise. Formulation of plans for financial and physical restructuring has proceeded more slowly, with greater focus being placed on more profitable enterprises. In part, this is because of inadequate skilled manpower at the disposal of the IPFs and that much attention was also being devoted to their participation in the second wave of privatization. A common perception, however, is that the close links of some large IPFs to banks may be slowing down the process of enterprise restructuring and that current disclosure rules do not impose sufficient market discipline on these funds. The Government is now reviewing the IPFs and commercial laws, including possible means to strengthen existing requirements for disclosure of financial results of both IPFs and companies.[18]

Monetary Policy and Financial Sector Reform

Since the introduction of reforms in early 1991, monetary policy has played a key role in financial stabilization of the economy. The reduction in inflation, stability of the nominal exchange rate, and the strengthening of the external reserves position attest to its success. The success is all the more impressive given the challenging environment in which policy has had to be implemented. Disruptions and uncertainties associated with systemic shocks, the short period of time since the introduction of reforms, and change in underlying behavioral relationships all made formulation of the appropriate policy stance difficult.

---

[18]Measures under consideration include the following requirements from publicly traded companies: issuing six-month reports, providing frequent information on the market value of portfolios, revealing the names and holdings of shareholders whose stake exceeds 5 percent, and releasing the fees or salaries of directors.

Monetary Policy Developments

Monetary and credit conditions in early 1991 turned out to be considerably tighter than planned, owing both to the higher-than-expected initial price jump and cautious lending behavior of banks. As the macroeconomic situation stabilized in the second half of 1991, monetary conditions were gradually eased to support economic recovery.

In the latter part of 1992 and early 1993, the conduct of monetary policy was complicated by the uncertainties associated with the dissolution of the former CSFR and the impending termination of the monetary union with Slovakia. Throughout this period, the authorities kept monetary policy on a tight leash. In the period immediately preceding and following the termination of the monetary union, monetary policy focused on eliminating the excess bank liquidity that arose from the large-scale conversion of currency holdings into bank deposits. The policy stance was eased in mid-1993, following several months of favorable external and inflation performance. In the succeeding 12 months, money expanded at a rapid pace—fueled primarily by the strengthening net foreign assets position—and the income velocity of broad money fell sharply. However, with signs of inflationary pressures building up, efforts to tighten monetary expansion were initiated in the third quarter of 1994.

Given a fixed exchange rate regime, strong capital inflows are creating increasing strains on the central bank in the conduct of monetary policy. Since mid-1993, foreign capital inflows have been the sole source of increase in reserve money. Although the task of monetary control has been facilitated by strong fiscal performance and the net creditor position of the National Property Fund (NPF), the Czech National Bank (CNB) has borne the main responsibility for sterilizing capital inflows. However, the CNB has been occasionally reluctant to sterilize too aggressively through open market operations because of the high cost of such operations and increasing evidence that sterilization was becoming less effective.

Czech policymakers have made considerable progress in developing indirect instruments of monetary control. With the removal of direct ceilings on commercial bank credits by October 1992, the primary focus of monetary control shifted to auctions of refinance credit and adjustments in minimum reserve requirements. Since mid-1993, the use of refinance credit auctions has been minimal and, with growing foreign capital inflows, open market operations have become increasingly important. In 1994, the system of monetary management has been based on open market operations, changes in reserve requirements, and, mainly to signal the intended policy stance to commercial banks, adjustments of the discount rate.

Reform of the Banking Sector

The establishment of a healthy commercial banking sector has figured prominently in the transformation program of the former CSFR during 1991–92 and subsequently in the Czech Republic. The efforts to this end have included the introduction of a more effective banking regulation and supervisory regime, the establishment of an efficient payments system, and strengthening the balance sheets of the commercial banks through a combination of both centralized and decentralized approaches.

The centralized operations were aimed at nonperforming loans inherited from the days of central planning or incurred on behalf of the state. The measures, which have been spread over time, have included transfers of debt out of individual banks, exchanging poor quality debt for official assets, and providing capital infusion. Excluding debt transfers where assets and matching liabilities were assumed by the Government or the Consolidation Bank (an agency initially set up specifically to clean up the balance sheets of commercial banks, but subsequently converted into a universal bank), total net contributions to banks by the authorities of the former CSFR and the Czech Republic amounted to Kč 132 billion at mid-1994 (equivalent to about 25 percent of bank credit outstanding just prior to the introduction of reforms). Receipts of privatization revenues from the NPF have been an important source for covering these costs.[19]

The decentralized approach requires banks to bear a major responsibility in accumulating loan-loss provisions and building up their capital base. To facilitate this task, the Government has given limited tax incentives for loan-loss provisions and issued risk classification guidelines and regulations covering credit exposures and capital adequacy. To minimize the moral hazard issues associated with the balance sheet restructuring operations and to strengthen corporate governance of banks, all the large formerly state-owned banks, with the exception of the foreign trade banks, were privatized in the first wave of voucher privatization. The state—through the NPF—retained between 37 and 53 percent of the shares, and the remainder was distributed through the voucher process. To foster competition, a liberal approach was taken to the entry of new private banks. Forty-seven new banks have emerged since the beginning of the reform process, about one half with partial or full foreign participation.

Notwithstanding the progress made in recent years, the banking system still suffers from inefficiencies and is fragile. A major deficiency is the limited maturity transformation by domestic banks, which has encouraged enterprises to borrow abroad. Domestic bank lending in recent years has been mainly short and medium term. Long-term credit (i.e., more than four years) has declined in absolute terms, and its share in total credit fell from 50 percent at the beginning of 1991 to about 30 percent at the end of 1993 and remained at this level in 1994. The reluctance of domestic banks to lend long term reflects their unwillingness to accept a significant mismatch between the maturity structure of their liabilities and assets. Bank deposits also are concentrated in short-term maturities. In 1993, 88 percent of new deposits were either in the form of demand deposits or maturities of less than one year, while total long-term deposits accounted for less than 7 percent of all deposits.[20]

Inefficiency in bank intermediation is also evidenced in the spread between deposit and lending rates: the average spread during 1992–94 generally has been between 6 and 8 percent. The wide spreads likely reflect the banks' burden of carrying nonperforming loans in their portfolios and the task of setting aside loan-loss provisions from net profits. With the recent introduction of a stricter and mandatory reporting system, about 38 percent of bank credit was reported as nonperforming at the end of December 1994, despite the support already provided for the cleaning of bank portfolios.[21] The big banks are reasonably provisioned and close to conformity with international supervisory norms, but the small banks have experienced a significant deterioration in the quality of their portfolios, are undercapitalized and do not have adequate loan-loss provisions. In early 1994, three small banks were placed under the special administration of the central bank, and several more began to be closely monitored. To help deal with the situation more effectively, a number of steps were initiated: amendments were made to the banking law to strengthen the supervisory powers of the central bank, and a deposit insurance scheme that covers all banks was introduced.

---

[19]These operations are described in detail in Bélanger and others (1995).

[20]One reason for this behavior may be that individuals, used to only short-term saving instruments available under central planning, have been slow to respond to the increasing range of longer-term bank instruments, notwithstanding the relatively higher rates of return. It is also possible that depositors wish to remain liquid to take advantage of other investment opportunities; for example, the stock market after it becomes better established.

[21]This estimate should be interpreted with caution as it is not risk weighted. On a risk-weighted basis, 24 percent of bank credit was nonperforming at the end of December 1994.

Fiscal Policy and Reforms

The objective of fiscal policy has been twofold: to reduce the role of the state in the economy and to help stabilize the economy. With the former objective in mind, the Government has implemented the following measures:

- Drastic cuts in subsidies in 1991 and keeping the level unchanged in nominal terms thereafter.

- Reform of corporate income taxation. In 1991, the rates of tax on profits were reduced by 10–20 percentage points and the rate structure was simplified. In 1993, a single tax on profits, with a 45 percent rate, replaced three earlier business taxes. The rate was lowered to 42 percent in 1994.

- Introduction of a sweeping tax reform in 1993, which included introduction of the VAT (at three rates of zero, 5, and 23 percent) and a reform of the income tax (both personal and corporate) and social security systems. A personal income tax on a progressive scale was introduced to replace the previous patchwork of taxes on the wages of large enterprises and various other forms of income. For social security, the old payroll tax of differential rates was replaced by a system where both the employer and the employee contributed.

The tax reforms of 1993 shifted the tax burden from corporate incomes onto wage incomes. Apart from reduced tax rates, additional incentives were provided to the enterprise sector through acceleration of allowed depreciation and tax credit for investment in selected equipment. The new system of VAT-cum-excises expanded the coverage of indirect taxes to services, mitigated the cascading implicit in the earlier turnover tax, and condensed the range of standard tax rates.

On the expenditure side, a number of social safety net programs were introduced in 1990. These included unemployment insurance, support of families in poverty and long-term unemployed, and cash payments to households in compensation for price liberalization. In 1994, programs of aid to low-income tenants and matching subsidies of voluntary, supplemental pension contributions in private plans were introduced. Barring these efforts, the entitlement system—especially, pensions and family allowances—continued to be as before under central planning.

The size of the fiscal balance and the extent of the government disengagement distinguish the experience of the former CSFR and the Czech Republic from that of other formerly planned economies during the initial years of transition. The government budget, as in other transition economies, came under considerable strain following the introduction of reforms. Nevertheless, the Government of the former CSFR managed to contain fiscal deficits to 2 percent of GDP in 1991 and 3½ percent of GDP in 1992. The fiscal accounts for the Czech Republic posted a small surplus in both 1993 and 1994 (Table 2.2).

Revenue as a ratio to GDP in the former CSFR fell by about 9 percentage points during 1991.[22] A part of the decline was related to the contraction of tax bases for profit tax, wage-related taxes, and domestic indirect taxes (profits, wages, and domestic consumption had all declined) that accompanied the reforms. A more important contributory factor, however, in sharp contrast to other transition economies, was the discretionary cuts in the rates for corporate income tax and turnover taxes.[23] The revenue-GDP ratio stabilized in 1992, and in the Czech Republic in 1993, it rose slightly (compared with the underlying position for the Czech lands in the previous year). This development primarily reflects reversal of some of the earlier endogenous revenue losses. In particular, an increase in real wages boosted wage-related taxes (mainly social insurance contributions). This compensated for the continuing decline in corporate income tax relative to GDP, arising from both discretionary action and endogenous factors. Although real consumption grew in 1992–93, there was no improvement in the share of indirect tax revenues in GDP. This reflects deficiencies in tax administration, especially the inability to capture a significant proportion of the increase in private economic activity.

The most salient feature of the trend in government expenditure is the sharp contraction of subsidies, which fell from 16 percent in the 1990 CSFR to less than 4 percent of GDP in the 1993 Czech Republic. Most of the reduction took place in 1991, as price liberalization removed many of the subsidies implicit in the administrative price structure.[24] The Czech authorities also have been successful in containing the other major components of expenditures. The ratios to GDP of current spending on goods and services and of transfers to households have been broadly maintained around 23–25 percent and 13 percent, respectively, since the introduction of the reform program. Transfer payments have been limited by the

---

[22]For the "available" general government; that is, not including interindustry transfers conducted through the funds of the ministries (eliminated in 1990) and gross operations of the subsidized organizations.

[23]Factors underlying the weakening performance of tax revenues in the various East European countries are analyzed in a recent study by Bélanger (1994).

[24]Currently, subsidies are devoted mainly to traditional sectors, such as agriculture and mining, and to maintaining prices of central heating and public transportation at below average cost.

Table 2.2. Major Components of Operations of the General Government in the Former Czech and Slovak Federal Republic and the Czech Republic[1]
(In percent of GDP)

	Former CSFR			Czech Republic	
	1990	1991	1992	1993	1994 (Prelim.)
Revenues	**60.1**	**51.5**	**51.6**	**50.5**	**49.4**
Profits tax	12.5	13.7	11.7	7.8	6.2
Personal income tax	6.7	6.1	7.7	3.3	5.3
Turnover tax (1990–92)/VAT and excise	18.0	12.6	12.8	11.8	12.8
Payroll tax (1990–92)/social insurance contributions	14.4	11.0	10.3	16.5	17.3
Expenditures	**60.0**	**53.4**	**55.2**	**50.0**	**50.7**
Consumption expenditures[2]	23.5	22.5	25.0	24.3	25.1
Interest	0.2	0.5	1.1	1.6	1.4
Transfers to households	13.7	16.1	16.4	13.3	13.6
Current transfers to enterprises	15.7	7.6	5.2	3.9	3.4
Capital expenditure and net lending	6.8	6.7	7.5	6.8	7.1
Balance without privatization revenues	**0.1**	**−2.0**	**−3.6**	**0.6**	**−1.3**
Use of privatization revenues[3]	—	—	—	0.8	1.8
Balance	**0.1**	**−2.0**	**−3.6**	**1.4**	**0.5**

Sources: National authorities; and IMF staff estimates.
[1]Includes central and local governments (budgetary and extrabudgetary operations), the National Health Fund, and the extrabudgetary funds (except NPF), but excludes funds of ministries and gross operations of subsidized organizations.
[2]Includes expenditures on goods and services, transfers to subsidized organizations, and expenditures of the National Health Fund.
[3]Includes only privatization revenues provided to the Government by the NPF to finance budgetary and quasi-budgetary operations.

comparatively mild degree of open unemployment and by a tightening of the eligibility requirements for the new programs of unemployment benefits and compensatory income support. In addition, the benefits of traditional programs, especially child allowances and pensions, were only partially indexed to inflation on a discretionary basis, while the increase in the number of pensioners was relatively small.[25] Unlike other transition countries, the Czech Republic has not had to face the pressure of debt-service payments, thanks to its low initial level of public debt.

From 1994, the government budget is being formulated within the framework of a medium-term strategy to achieve the following objectives: reduce the expenditure-to-GDP ratio gradually to 40–42 percent by the year 2000, reduce the tax burden to levels prevailing in industrial countries, and stabilize the nominal level of public debt. As a part of the latter consideration, the objective is to achieve a balanced budget every year.[26] Fiscal pressures

loom ahead, however, in part because of higher expenditure claims of social benefits. It is the intention of the authorities to restore some of the erosion of pensions in real terms. In addition, both the pension system and health care will face the burden of an aging population, which, at the turn of the century, will cause the ratio of the old to young to increase. To contain these costs, the authorities have started to prepare fundamental reform measures that will address some of the shortcomings of the social security system and other elements of the social safety net. Presently, the structure of transfers is complex, with overlaps between programs. The transfer programs inherited from the days of central planning are deficient in many respects, including minimal redistributional transfers according to means of recipients, virtually no link between contributions and benefits in transfers of a social insurance nature, and almost no use of prices to allocate in-kind transfers, such as health care and education. Pension reforms are scheduled for implementation in mid-1995. Reforms of present state benefits (family allowances, compensatory income support) and general assistance are scheduled for 1996.

---

[25]The number of pensioners in the Czech lands increased by about 5 percent during 1991–93, far more slowly than in Poland.
[26]See Ministry of Finance (1994).

Tasks and Challenges Ahead

The Czech transformation process has now entered a new stage. The major tasks in this phase are to consolidate the gains of stabilization and press ahead with restructuring of enterprises. The rebound of economic activity, strong export performance, strong capital inflows in the form of enterprise borrowing abroad, and increasing nonperforming loans in the portfolio of domestic banks suggest dualism in the industrial sector, with some firms already making necessary adjustments and doing well but others continuing to struggle through the transformation process. For enterprise restructuring to accelerate, the IPFs—the new owners of companies privatized through the voucher scheme—will have to force the pace. Making the IPFs increasingly accountable to their own shareholders through regular and timely disclosure of information would be effective in ensuring that they efficiently manage the enterprises in their portfolios.

It is doubtful that the envisaged transformation of the economy can be achieved without substantial enterprise closures. Rigidities and distortions that are still built into the economy will also need to be eliminated. Unless measures are urgently taken to improve labor mobility from areas of surplus labor to places where new jobs are being created, not only is it likely that regional unemployment from firm closures will be high but also economic growth will be stifled. A chronic shortage of housing currently constrains labor mobility. Priority, therefore, has to be given to accelerating the pace of rent decontrol and taking other measures to attract investment in housing.

Until investment and imports have picked up sufficiently, growing capital inflows are likely to continue posing a dilemma for monetary management. To help alleviate the problems created by capital flows, the authorities have already begun initiatives to eliminate the residual restrictions on external current account transactions and introduce limited additional liberalization of the capital account. The functioning of the financial system clearly needs to be improved, with much of the capital inflows reflecting insufficient maturity transformation and inefficient intermediation by the domestic banking system. Current regulations limit the room for provisioning from pretax profits and treat accrued but unpaid interest on bad loans as taxable income increase the costs of financial intermediation. Removing these distortions should lower interest rate spreads and the domestic cost of capital, thereby reducing the incentive for capital inflows.

References

Aghevli, B.B., E. Borensztein, and T. van der Willigen, *Stabilization and Structural Reform in the Czech and Slovak Federal Republic: First Stage*, IMF Occasional Paper, No. 92 (Washington: International Monetary Fund, March 1992).

Baldwin, Richard E., *Towards an Integrated Europe* (London: Centre for Economic Policy Research, 1994).

Bélanger, Gérard, "Eastern Europe—Factors Underlying the Weakening Performance of Tax Revenues," IMF Working Paper, WP/94/104 (Washington, September 1994).

_____, and others, *Czech Republic*, IMF Economic Reviews, No. 1 (Washington: International Monetary Fund, April 1995).

Borensztein, E., D.G. Demekas, and J. Ostry, "The Output Decline in the Aftermath of Reform: The Cases of Bulgaria, Czechoslovakia, and Romania," IMF Working Paper, WP/92/59 (Washington: International Monetary Fund, July 1992).

Čapek, Aleš, "Output Decline and the Dynamics of Privatization in the Czech Republic," paper presented at a conference at the International Institute for Applied Systems Analysis (IIASA), Laxenburg, Austria, November 1993.

Dyba, K. and J. Svejnar, "Stabilization and Transition in Czechoslovakia," in *The Transition in Eastern Europe*, ed. by O. Blanchard, K. Froot, and J. Sachs, Vol. 1 (Chicago: University of Chicago Press, 1994), pp. 93–123.

Ham, John, Jan Svejnar, and Katherine Terrell, "The Czech and Slovak Labor Markets During the Transition," CERGE Working Paper (Prague: Charles University, Center for Economic Research and Graduate Education, February 1994).

Ministry for the Administration of National Property and Its Privatization, *Report on the Privatization Process for the Years 1989 to 1992* (Prague, 1993).

Ministry of Finance, *Transformation and Fiscal Policy in the Czech Republic* (Prague, 1994).

OECD (1994a), *Industry in the Czech and Slovak Republics* (Paris, 1994).

_____(1994b), *Review of the Labour Market in the Czech Republic* (unpublished report of the Employment, Labour and Social Affairs Committee, Paris, 1994).

PlanEcon Report, Vol. VIII, Nos. 50–52 (Washington: December 1992).

Portes, Richard, "Transformation Traps," *The Economic Journal*, Vol. 104 (September 1994), pp. 1178–89.

Shafik, Nemat, "Making a Market: Mass Privatization in the Czech and Slovak Republics," Policy Research Working Paper, No. 1231 (Washington: World Bank, December 1993).

Šujan, I., and M. Šujanova, "The Macroeconomic Situation in the Czech Republic," Working Paper No. 46 (Prague: Charles University, Center for Economic Research and Graduate Education, April 1994).

Tůma, Zdeněk, "Economic Restructuring and Corporate Insolvency Procedures in the Czech Economy," paper presented at an OECD conference held in Vienna, September 28–30, 1994.

III Developments and Challenges in Hungary

Mark S. Lutz and Thomas H. Krueger

In contrast to other previously centrally planned countries in Central and Eastern Europe, Hungary has always been distinguished by the "gradualist" approach it has taken toward economic and institutional reforms. Its "goulash" communism was the label given to an economic system that, while retaining central planning, allowed for significant enterprise autonomy. In many respects, this served the population well and shortages were largely absent. Moreover, decisions to keep domestic relative prices close to their international counterparts since the early 1980s implied that the degree of enterprise restructuring thought to be necessary was less than in other members of the former Council for Mutual Economic Assistance (CMEA).

On the other hand, the gradualist approach has resulted in recurrent macroeconomic imbalances. The lack of adjustment in response to the first oil price shock contributed to the initial buildup of international debt. Similarly, recurrent excessive demand throughout the 1980s led the authorities to reverse previous attempts at liberalization. Moreover, following the return of democratically elected governments in 1990, failures to undertake significant reforms in the excessively broad and actuarially unsound system of social expenditures as well as in reducing the scope and scale of governmental activities, has resulted recently in the re-emergence of substantial fiscal and external imbalances.

Nonetheless, Hungary has, in many areas, completed necessary structural and institutional reforms. This is reflected, among other things, in a fairly vibrant private sector (even more so if the underground economy is included) and in foreign direct investment equivalent to over half of the total amount in the region. Nevertheless, significant structural reforms and, more immediate though interrelated, macroeconomic measures are necessary to place the economy on a sustainable path of high growth.

Structural Reforms

Of all the transition economies, Hungary was the first to introduce, in 1968, market-oriented reforms.

Many were reversed, however, or, as the theory of second-best suggests, led to inconsistencies with other yet-to-be reformed features of the economy. As a result, economic efficiency remained low throughout the 1970s and 1980s. Reform efforts were broadened in the late 1980s and further accelerated under the first freely elected government in forty years, and the later reform efforts constitute the main focus of this section.

Pre-1990 Reforms

A process of market-oriented reforms began in Hungary in 1968, with the adoption of the New Economic Mechanism (NEM), and encompassed three distinct liberalizing periods.[1] The first, covering roughly 1968–73, entailed a substantial broadening of enterprise autonomy in decision making within the national plan. However, a lack of reforms in other areas, as well as growing political and social tensions, led to reregulation of the economy in the mid- to late 1970s. The 1970s ended with a renewed attempt at liberalization of enterprise decision making, as well as a broad alignment of domestic relative prices with their international counterparts. But continued soft budget constraints again resulted in macroeconomic imbalances, including further increases in external debt levels. These, in turn, led to a reimposition of direct controls.

A third, and under the communist regime final, attempt at market-oriented reforms began in the latter half of the 1980s. In many respects these reforms were the broadest based and most ambitious, embracing substantial institutional reforms, as well as legal and regulatory dimensions. While they embraced social and political, as well as economic spheres, the most important among the latter related to fiscal reforms, restructuring of the banking sector, and changes in enterprise structure and governance.

---

[1] For further details, see Berend and Ránki (1985), Boote and Somogyi (1991), and, regarding fiscal reforms, Kopits (1993) and Lutz (1992).

Fiscal Reforms

While Hungary has almost continuously implemented marginal adjustments in tax and expenditure policies, prior to the mid-1980s fiscal policy was in general simply a tool for implementing the financial counterpart to the central plan. Thereafter, the authorities initiated reforms in public finances in a number of areas, including tax simplification and reform, early steps toward reductions in subsidies, and initial efforts to improve transparency, openness, and public accountability of the budget process.

Hungary was the first country in transition to institute a system of taxation consistent with a market economy. In 1988, a value-added tax with three rates, zero, 15, and 25 percent, was adopted. It was buttressed by a number of significant excises, focusing on motor fuels, alcohol, and some luxury goods. Regarding the taxation of personal income, the implicit taxation through rigid wage and interest rate controls was replaced in the early 1980s by taxes on incomes from the second economy,[2] and in 1988 by a narrowly based tax primarily on wage income, and withholding taxes on dividend and interest incomes. A uniform parametric tax on enterprise profits was adopted in 1989, replacing the highly discretionary and invasive taxation of firms' cash flows and various funds. Nevertheless, a large number of tax reliefs, mainly through reduced statutory rates, continued to exist to reward or induce particular activities.

Hungary, like other countries in Eastern Europe, made extensive use of subsidies to households and enterprises through the budget, through low fixed prices for basic commodities and services, and through selective access to foreign exchange and domestic credits at preferential rates. Efforts were undertaken in the 1980s to increase and later to liberalize prices to reflect their international counterparts.[3] Interest rate liberalization necessitated budgetizing what had previously been largely a quasi-fiscal subsidy for mortgage subsidies.

The structure of government became de facto increasingly decentralized throughout the 1980s.[4]

Facing steadily increasing financing pressures, the Government allowed central budgetary institutions greater latitude to collect, retain and determine the spending of own revenues. Beginning in 1986, budgets of local councils were separated from the state budget, with the latter ceding particular tax revenues and providing specified transfers to the former. As with central budgetary institutions, local councils' own revenues, which often were significant, could be spent without central guidance or carried over to the next year. In 1989, the social security budget was similarly separated.

Banking and Capital Market Reforms

In contrast to reforms in other areas, the New Economic Mechanism left the banking sector with the subordinated role of financing the national plan. Aside from a few specialized financial institutions, the National Bank of Hungary (NBH) was responsible for both central and commercial banking functions, as well as regulating foreign exchange operations and acting as the nation's official borrower.[5] It also directly controlled credit allocation, as interest rates played only a marginal allocative role, and indirect monetary policy instruments were absent.

In general, financial savings were low. Households did not have a strong incentive to save, given virtually guaranteed employment and the provision of many services either by the state or through enterprises and a limited choice of consumer durables. Moreover, households generally faced negative real interest rates and a limited portfolio of saving instruments. Enterprises preferred physical investments, which were either self-financed or used government loans and grants or bank credit, in part because of a pattern of confiscation by the authorities of profitable enterprises' accumulated financial assets.

---

[2]The second economy consisted of small shops, restaurants, and separate units within large enterprises, which provided goods and services to the latter, using the latter's assets.

[3]In this context it should be noted that the state budget made use of extensive subsidies and taxes on goods traded with Hungary's CMEA partners so that domestic producers would find such trade to be as rewarding as engaging in production for domestic sale or for exports to the West.

[4]At the central government level, there are budgetary chapters, comprising the spending ministries, offices of the President and Prime Minister, Parliament, and other agencies. Attached to these chapters are central budgetary institutions amounting to 1,395 at the end of 1993. In addition, a large number of extrabudgetary funds

exist and are administered by the budgetary chapters. The social insurance system is also at the central government level. The general government includes the central government as well as local governments, or, as they were referred to in the 1980s, local councils. General government financial flows are also quite decentralized, with extensive transactions among the various components of the central and general government. As a result, and given an inadequate reporting system, the recorded level of fiscal activity is thought to be significantly overstated.

[5]Specialized financial institutions included the State Development Bank (in charge of financing large investments), the Foreign Trade Bank (financing foreign currency trade), the National Savings Bank (NSB), the postal savings network, and savings cooperatives (the latter three financing household mortgages). In general, household monetary and credit flows were separated from those of the enterprise sector, and financial intermediation outside of the budget remained limited.

While monetary policy accommodated the National Plan's projected inflation rates, the latter remained fairly low until the late 1980s. However, the periodic tightening of credits during periods of excess aggregate demand, the virtual guaranteed granting of credits for working capital purposes to ensure the payment of wages (and the resulting weakening of enterprise financial discipline), and the periodic financing of intra-enterprise arrears by perennial loss-making enterprises left the balance sheet of the NBH, as well as of the State Development Bank, with large amounts of impaired loans.

As the authorities became increasingly aware of the problems posed by the financial system, several institutional reforms were implemented. In 1987, a two-tier banking system was introduced, with the domestic commercial banking operations of the NBH and State Development Bank taken over by three new commercial banks, although the latter remained owned by the state and state enterprises. These banks inherited the loans (both good and bad) and deposits of their predecessors; and the Foreign Trade Bank was also allowed to provide commercial banking services. A number of joint venture banks with foreign participation were also created. Also in that year, banks were allowed to use interest rates to compete for enterprise deposits. In 1988–89, banks were granted additional rights to provide foreign exchange related services to their clients.

As regards the household financial sphere, in 1989 the Government halted the issuance of low interest rate (at most 3 percent) mortgages to households, replacing them with standard mortgages, with one-time capital grants, and interest subsidies financed by the budget. The outstanding stock of below-market mortgages was purchased from the NSB with bonds paying market-related interest rates and transferred to a newly created extrabudgetary fund. This allowed the NSB to pay higher deposit rates, although ceilings remained in place.

With the creation of the two-tier banking system, the NBH gradually shifted from direct credit ceilings to the use of indirect monetary instruments. It instituted refinancing quotas, and increasingly relied on interest rate policy as a principal instrument of monetary control. The latter became more flexible in 1988 with the auctioning of treasury bills. The NBH established a system of prudential regulations and banking supervision and imposed a system of reserve requirements.

Enterprise Structure and Governance

Amendments to the State Enterprise Act of 1975, which took effect January 1, 1985, established a new institutional framework for state enterprises based upon self-management with worker participation. However, continued poor enterprise performance, the result of a lack of effective exercise of ownership rights, soft budget constraints, and the continued periodic interference by central authorities, motivated the introduction of the Law on Transformation in 1989, which sought to provide the legal framework for transforming state enterprises and cooperatives into joint-stock companies. Attempts to regularize the privatization process also began, in response to growing popular resentment over "spontaneous" privatization of state assets initiated by enterprises. This included the adoption in 1988 of the Act on Foreign Investment, which codified rights and obligations for foreign investors, as well as allowing for the formation of wholly foreign-owned enterprises.

In 1989, the Law on Association provided for greater freedom in forming a variety of corporate entities, as well as permitting individuals to acquire stakes in state enterprises, and established liberal rules for foreign joint-venture activities. Combined with trade liberalization, relating to both import licensing, as well as freedom of enterprises to directly engage in foreign trade, it was hoped that increased competition would result.

Attempts were also made to further improve enterprise governance. Multiyear restructuring plans were adopted in a number of sectors and a bankruptcy law was adopted in 1986. The latter, however, relied on negotiations between creditors and debtors for out-of-court settlements of claims. If unsuccessful, the Ministry of Finance would determine if state-financed restructuring was necessary, in light of regional employment, national defense, or external trade commitments. If not, as a last resort, court proceedings could be initiated. As a result of this protracted process, few significant proceedings were actually initiated.

Reforms Since 1990

With the end of the socialist era in 1990, numerous economic and social challenges came to the forefront. While, as seen above, efforts had been made previously to adapt the system of central planning to increase its responsiveness, wholesale changes were needed to make activities consistent with a market economy, including changes in enterprise structure and governance, and in labor and capital markets. Moreover, a number of the previous reforms, including trade and price liberalization, and those relating to the budget, tax policy, and the banking system, needed to be further extended and refined.

The incoming government formulated a broad-based, four-year plan for structural and macroeconomic reforms during its first year in office. The so-called Kupa program, named after the Minister of Finance, spelled out a detailed plan, specifying the problems to be addressed, the intended goals, the necessary tasks of the government, the forms of remedy (laws, regulations, creation of new institutions), their scheduled dates of enactment or creation, and the relevant government institutions responsible.[6]

Success with structural reforms has been uneven. Considerable progress was achieved with respect to price and trade liberalization, where the Hungarian economy now enjoys a relatively liberal system. On the other hand, progress has proven more difficult in many areas of fiscal reform, as well as enterprise and bank restructuring. As a result, the state's continued pervasive role, including in its redistributive function with associated high marginal tax rates, has hampered economic activity and, more generally, contributed to the macroeconomic tensions currently facing the Hungarian economy.

Price Liberalization

As already noted, the pricing system had been liberalized in stages since 1968. By 1989, only 17 percent of consumer prices remained "flexible," that is, fixed unless officially adjusted, with the remainder freely determined.[7] The share of free consumer prices was increased to 89 percent in 1991, 92 percent in 1992, and 94 percent in 1993.[8] Government-determined prices remain only for electric energy, public transport, and pharmaceuticals. In 1991, the Price Office, which was responsible for controlling prices, was eliminated.

Trade Liberalization

The new government was the leading international advocate of dismantling the CMEA trading system. Compared with 1987, in which 49 percent of exports and 47 percent of imports were settled in transferable rubles, the corresponding figures had already declined in 1990 to 26 percent and 29 percent, respectively. This in part reflected the inability of the former Soviet Union to fulfill its obligations in energy exports. Moreover, the nation had recorded significant surpluses in its nonconvertible overall balance of payments in 1990–91, with limited expectations for transforming its accumulated surplus into valuable assets. The system was dismantled from 1991, with almost all transactions

thereafter being conducted at world prices and in convertible currencies.[9]

The newly elected government intended to align its trade policies with those of the European Community (EC) members. By 1991, about 90 percent of total imports were free of quantitative or value limitations. Moreover, in early 1992, an association agreement was adopted with the EC, mandating an asymmetric timetable for the dismantling of trade barriers. Also, the Central European Free Trade Agreement (CEFTA), comprising Hungary, Poland, the Czech and Slovak Republics, and subsequently Slovenia, was adopted, including a timetable for a free-trade area among its partners. At the beginning of 1995, further trade liberalization was implemented under agreements with the European Union (EU), CEFTA, and the European Free Trade Association (EFTA), as well as under the Uruguay Round.

Fiscal Reforms

The reform program included an ambitious strategy to modify the budgetary sector to make it consistent with a market economy.[10] This included further reforming the tax system, reducing the scope and scale of fiscal activities, and increasing the efficiency of remaining activities. While partial but significant progress was made on the first objective, the other two were largely not achieved.

Regarding tax reforms, the Government intended to broaden direct tax bases by reducing and eliminating the large number of tax reliefs and exemptions granted under enterprise profit and personal income taxation. In addition, it intended to introduce realistic depreciation rates and to eliminate the zero bracket in the value-added tax (VAT).

To this end, new laws were adopted in 1992 on accounting, which, inter alia, allowed institutions to adopt more realistic depreciation rates, and tax reform, which resulted in a significant leveling and broadening of effective enterprise profit tax rates across sectors.[11] However, measures to broaden personal income tax and social security contribution bases were not adopted. Moreover, VAT reforms were delayed until fiscal pressures dominated in January 1993. At that time, the zero bracket was eliminated (with minor exceptions)

---

[6]Refer to Ministry of Finance (1991a) and (1991b).

[7]The share of freely determined producer prices was 77 percent.

[8]The share of free producer prices was raised to 93 percent in 1991.

[9]As noted above, the Government had instituted a system of taxes on and subsidies to enterprises engaged in trade with CMEA partners such that sales to domestic or convertible currency markets were equally profitable. As a result, the shift to trade at world prices resulted in a loss of net fiscal revenues of about 2 percent of GDP, compared with similar or greater losses at the enterprise level in other Eastern European countries.

[10]For a more extensive discussion of these issues, see Lutz (1994a).

[11]See Lutz (1994c).

and the 15 percent bracket was replaced by a two-bracket, 8 and 25 percent, system. Similar pressures necessitated an increase in the lower rate to 10 percent from August 1993 and to 12 percent from January 1995.

As to the intended goal to reduce the scope and scale of governmental activities, the authorities were even less ambitious and successful, compared with their stated intentions. The share of general government expenditure is estimated at around 60 percent of GDP in 1993/94, a higher share than at the beginning of the reform process in 1990 and also considerably higher than in most of the other transition economies in Central Europe. It should be noted, however, that the reduction in subsidies to producers and consumers was followed through as intended. In spite of budgetizing previous quasi-fiscal subsidies related to below-market interest rates charged on housing mortgages, the Government reduced overall subsidies from an amount equivalent to 12.2 percent of GDP in 1990 to a budgeted 5.3 percent of GDP in 1994. The composition has also changed radically: all consumer subsidies were eliminated except those related to transportation, while agricultural subsidies increased (in part due to significant droughts in recent years).

Regarding other aspects of government activity, the authorities ultimately failed to carry out many of their stated intentions. The new budgetary framework law, adopted in June 1992, failed to address the fundamental weaknesses in the structure of government. In this regard, three areas in particular illustrate the weakness of structural reforms in the fiscal domain.

First, the new budgetary framework law of 1992 continued to allow decentralized central (and local) budgetary institutions freedom to collect and spend own revenues without central supervision and to allow the same to maintain independent bank accounts and purchase treasury paper, and it failed to institute centralized treasury (i.e., cash and debt management) operations. This has limited control of budgetary operations, including the ability to adjust fiscal behavior during the year as may become warranted by unexpected developments.

Second, despite the Government's stated goals, no serious efforts were undertaken to create a timely and comprehensive fiscal information system and to evaluate the activities of government institutions in light of their consistency with a market economy. Given that the Government employs (including those in health and education) some 25 percent of the workforce, there is a clear need to undertake a wholesale re-evaluation and reduction in public sector activities and employment. Moreover, many central (and local) budgetary institutions are engaged either primarily or secondarily in providing commer-cial goods and services. Therefore, the need for a wholesale re-examination of the role of government remains unanswered.

The third area concerns the presently large and unsustainable level of social expenditures. In spite of combined social insurance contributions equivalent to 60.8 percent of the wage bill, among the highest in the world and with deleterious effects for factor market efficiency and external competitiveness, the pension system remains actuarially unsound.[12] Moreover, despite a government-prepared white paper in 1991 stating the need for increases in pension ages, they have yet to be increased. In addition, family allowances remain among the most generous in Europe and are not means tested (although the Government, in mid-March 1995, presented a package that would include a switch to means testing later in 1995). Also, pharmaceutical subsidies, which exceed 1 percent of GDP, remain a nagging area for reform.

Monetary Policy and Banking Reforms

Reforms initiated by the previous regime concerning the conduct of monetary policy and the regulation and structure of the banking system have continued. While the National Bank of Hungary turned increasingly toward the use of indirect monetary instruments, the effectiveness of these instruments in transmitting their intentions was weakened by the reactions of commercial banks to rapidly growing, nonperforming segments of their portfolios, and government guarantees and subsidized credits insulated important segments of the market from the effects of indirect monetary instruments.

The NBH has made steady progress in introducing and increasingly relying on indirect instruments to effect monetary policy. The practice of providing automatic refinancing credits was gradually replaced with a system of auctions. Moreover, the cost of such credits was progressively increased, to induce banks to compete for deposits. Ceilings on household deposit rates were eliminated by 1992. An interbank market, created in 1990, played an increasing role in supplying banks with marginal short-term funding. The NBH also streamlined, reduced, and began paying interest on banks' mandatory reserves.

A number of legal acts also directly influenced the structure and actions of the banking system. In December 1991, Parliament passed both central banking and commercial banking laws.[13] Among the more important features of the former are an explicit state-

---

[12] For a more complete description of the significantly damaging effects of increasing social insurance contributions, see Lutz (1994b).
[13] Concerning the former, refer to Ministry of Finance (1992a) and to National Bank of Hungary (1991). As for the commercial banking law, see Ministry of Finance (1992c).

ment concerning the NBH's legal independence; its primary responsibility for ensuring the value of the currency; and a stricter limit, to be phased in over a number of years, on the amount of direct financing of the state budget deficit.[14]

Regarding the latter legislation, one of its most important components was in requiring banks to provision out of pretax income for impaired or non-performing assets and to provision fully for all loans, whether performing or not, by firms under bankruptcy proceedings. This requirement, combined with stringent bankruptcy and modern accounting laws adopted in 1992, resulted in large increases in required provisioning. Banks, which had previously booked "phantom" incomes (from accrued but not paid interest receipts) and had paid tax liabilities on these, sharply increased interest spreads to generate necessary cash flows. Moreover, a surge in the number of firms in bankruptcy proceedings in early 1992 created a climate among banks that strongly discouraged new lending and refinancing loans falling due to creditworthy customers. As a result, significant nongovernmental financial disintermediation occurred, as banks instead chose to hold government paper or to maintain excess reserves with the NBH.

The Government increasingly recognized that it must take action both to improve the financial integrity of the banking system and to alter incentives such that banks would be willing to reduce operating spreads and resume lending to creditworthy customers. Mindful that it was in part responsible for the emergence of subsequent doubtful loans (e.g., by failing to shut down loss-making enterprises with large labor forces), the Government introduced the first loan consolidation scheme at the end of 1992. Under the scheme, government bonds were swapped for variable proportions of classified loans, depending upon their date of creation and whether the enterprises concerned were to remain in state hands. The scheme, however, was hastily prepared, insufficient in size, and contained a number of flaws. Despite increasing risks of moral hazard, a second scheme was adopted at the end of 1993, in which participating state-owned banks retained their doubtful loans but received capital injections in the form of interest-bearing government bonds. Under this program, the capital adequacy ratio of participating banks was increased to zero by the end of 1993, to 4 percent in mid-1994 and, for selected banks, to 8 percent by the end of 1994. Together, the amount of consolidation bonds issued by the state to banks under the various schemes amounted to some $7^1/_2$ percent of 1994 GDP. While this appears to have largely addressed

the "stock" problem concerning the banks' minimum capital adequacy, difficulties in fully altering incentives relating to bank lending behavior based upon sound banking principles continue.

Capital Market Reforms

In 1990, the Budapest Stock Market reopened, the first in the European countries in transition, after a more than forty-year hiatus. Within the following few years, a large number of acts supporting private capital markets were adopted.[15] An interbank market for foreign exchange was created in 1992, and a futures market for these assets was created the following year. Also, an act in 1993 established a bank-financed deposit insurance fund, and the adoption in 1994 of a law allowing for the creation of private pension schemes further strengthened and began to broaden capital markets in Hungary.[16]

Despite these measures, capital market developments to date have been rather lopsided. In part reflecting the privatization path chosen in Hungary, the number of enterprises listed on the stock exchange is rather limited. Moreover, trading activity in nonbank capital markets is dominated by government paper.[17] Nevertheless, activity in the private placement of commercial paper (and some bonds) has shown some growth and direct borrowing from abroad by well-known domestic or foreign joint-venture firms has grown substantially in the past three years.

Enterprise Governance and Structure

The Government was determined to accelerate the transformation of state enterprise behavior consistent with a market economy. This involved hardening budget constraints, instituting a broad-based privatization plan, and further increasing the autonomy granted to enterprise decision making. While the growing segment of privatized enterprises, combined with the explosion of de novo private ventures, soon accounted for the majority of activity, the economy continues to be hampered by persistent problems posed by a number of significant large loss-making state-owned enterprises.

The Government's subsidy reduction program, as well as the newly adopted accounting, auditing, bankruptcy, and commercial banking laws, all acted

---

[14]It should be noted that the Government undermined this independence by requiring in the 1994 budget law that the NBH directly finance an amount of the budget deficit in excess of that specified in the transitory provisions of the central banking law.

[15]For the Acts on Compensation, Accounting, Investment Funds and Employee Stock Ownership Plans, refer to Ministry of Finance (1991c), (1991d), (1992b), (1992c), and (1992d).

[16]See Ministry of Finance (1993).

[17]See Morgan (1993). The Ministry of Finance reports that in 1992–93 trading in government securities accounted for over 80 percent of total exchange activity.

to effectively harden budget constraints for the vast majority of private and state-owned enterprises. The Government built upon this foundation by adopting a privatization plan emphasizing the transferring of ownership rights to those who had significant incentives to either directly manage or actively monitor the actions of hired managers.[18]

Moreover, the Government acted to further increase the autonomy granted to managers of state-owned enterprises by abolishing in 1993 the system of excess wage taxation. With hardened budget constraints, and a newly adopted social safety net (including unemployment compensation and, subsequently, social assistance payments), it was thought that firms would retain only those employees necessary for profitable production.

The economic structure of production has changed dramatically since 1989. The number of economic organizations with legal entity has increased from 15,000 to 97,000 in September 1994, while the number of registered unincorporated businesses has increased from 245,000 to 766,000 during the same period (although some of the increase reflects a tax treatment that is more favorable for self-employed than for employees). Moreover, enterprises employing over 300 employees accounted for 19 percent of total legal economic organizations in 1989; in 1993, they accounted for only 1 percent. The number of newly created private and privatized economic organizations is estimated to have accounted for well over 50 percent of activity in 1994.

Nevertheless, the tightening of budget constraints, combined with the sharp fall in external and domestic demand and change in production and trade patterns, exposed a large number of state-owned enterprises as fundamentally unsound. While most small and medium-sized enterprises were forced to confront their situation through downsizing, bankruptcy, or liquidation proceedings, a number of large enterprises, employing significant shares of the labor force, were able to continue operating while accumulating large losses.[19] Plans are under way for enterprise restructuring and debtor consolidation concerning these enterprises; however, it is anticipated that this will result in substantial additional unemployment.

Labor Market Reforms

A number of significant reforms have taken place regarding labor issues in recent years. A system of centralized bargaining has been created, and institutions facilitating labor market mobility have emerged. The labor market, however, remains extremely inflexible, with little mobility between employment and unemployment, and within employment. Moreover, real wages appear to be excessively rigid, especially when nonwage compensation is taken into account.

A tripartite Interest Reconciliation Council (IRC), comprising representatives of trade unions, employers' organizations, and the government, was formed in 1988.[20] It was reorganized in 1990, and decisions now are made on the basis of consensus. While its main role remains consultative, its decisions in determining the minimum wage rates are taken as binding. These decisions serve as the basis for subsequent, less comprehensive, wage arrangements at industry and firm levels.

In the early 1990s, a number of institutions to promote labor mobility and provide a social safety net were created. The Solidarity Fund, which provides unemployment compensation, was created in 1991.[21] The Employment Fund, which had existed since the late 1980s, was enlarged, with greater emphasis placed on labor market information services and worker retraining. In 1992, a social assistance law was adopted, providing cash benefits and specific services for those that have either exhausted or are not eligible for unemployment compensation.

Some features of present labor market practices have hindered its smooth functioning. First, the centralized wage recommendation system through the IRC has de facto led to a tying of wage increases to increases in the minimum wage. Because the latter is

---

[18]The Government's privatization plan combined a quick "pre-privatization" of some 10,000 small service establishments and initially, following the above-mentioned negative reaction to previously attempted "spontaneous" privatization, a case-by-case decision process concerning larger enterprises. When the latter proved to be too slow, the privatization process was itself "privatized," allowing for state-approved private intermediaries to facilitate the process of bringing together potential owners and firms. In 1990, the Government created the State Property Agency (AVU), whose mandate was to privatize the enterprises within its portfolio. The State Asset Management Company (AV Rt) was formed in 1992 and was given control over about 150 enterprises in which the Government intended to retain a 100 percent, a majority, or a significant minority interest.

[19]At their peak in 1992, losses totaled Ft 415 billion, equivalent to 14.8 percent of GDP. The 41 largest loss-makers, which accounted for 4 percent of the total employment, lost over Ft 100 billion. It is thought that these losses were financed through a building up of arrears to the tax authorities, the social security system, and other enterprises, as well as through a decapitalization of the firms themselves.

[20]For a comprehensive description of recent labor relations in Hungary, see Plant (1993).

[21]The initial replacement rates and benefit periods provided to the unemployed in Hungary may have retarded job search incentives; subsequent reductions in both have brought these parameters within Western European norms.

so close to the calculated minimum subsistence wage, maintaining its real value may be justified. However, resulting general real wage rigidity has undoubtedly depressed the level of employment. Moreover, subsequent rounds of industry and firm-specific agreements exacerbate insider-outsider problems, disenfranchising the unemployed in influencing wage patterns, and inducing negative spill-over effects, thereby imparting an upward bias to wage patterns.[22]

Second, wage bargaining has paid insufficient attention to nonwage (e.g., fringe benefit) compensation, possibly because of continued soft budget constraints in many large state-owned enterprises, discussed in the previous section. However, in light of its exclusion from personal income and social insurance contribution bases, nonwage compensation has been the most rapidly growing form of compensation, accounting now for a substantial (over 20 percent) share in total compensation. Third, centralized bargaining has impeded geographic wage dispersion, which is sorely needed, given unemployment rates in the eastern half of the country that are double their western half counterparts. In many of these areas of labor market weakness, a contributing factor has been the role of large loss-making state-owned firms that have failed to exercise an effective voice for capital, inducing wage increases in excess of those suggested by micro- and macroeconomic circumstances.

Macroeconomic Performance

Hungary entered the postcommunist era in many respects in a relatively favorable position compared with its partner countries in Central and Eastern Europe. Aside from the above-mentioned history of progress toward economic liberalization in the structural area, favorable features included a less distortionary price system; a more stable internal macroeconomic position at the outset than in many other countries; a smaller, even though still dominant, share of external trade that was conducted within the CMEA trading bloc; a skilled labor force; and proximity to Western markets. On the other hand, Hungary was burdened by very high external debt levels that temporarily impeded private market access in the period of uncertainty surrounding other nation's halting of debt servicing and the changeover to the first freely elected postcommunist government.

Against this background of initial conditions, developments in external accounts were a focal point for macroeconomic developments in Hungary. Accordingly, one can divide the past five years or so into two broad episodes. First, a period of external stabilization during 1990–92 when the current account recorded small surpluses, access to external capital markets was re-established, and inflation rates declined following an initial, though by international comparison relatively small, upsurge. A second macroeconomic phase started already in late 1992, but became fully apparent in 1993–94. A deterioration in the private saving-investment balance was accompanied by high public sector dissaving and, as a result, the external current account deteriorated markedly. Moreover, progress toward lower inflation stalled. Throughout this period, employment fell sharply, and officially reported output contracted until 1994.

This section provides a selective overview of macroeconomic developments since 1990. It highlights factors underlying the output decline in 1990–93, and the inflation and external performance of the Hungarian economy. In this context, it becomes evident that a lack of progress in several areas of structural reform, as previously discussed, has also impeded macroeconomic stabilization and growth.

Output and Employment Performance

The cumulative fall in official GDP during the first years of adjustment—by about one fifth over 1990–93—was broadly similar in Hungary, Poland, and the Czech Republic. For Hungary, the sharp decline followed a decade of slow growth (about $1\frac{1}{2}$ percent a year) in spite of high investment-to-GDP ratios, which were partly financed by external borrowing. The first robust growth in GDP in seven years, estimated at some 2 percent, occurred in 1994 (Chart 3.1). The earlier output decline was accompanied by a broadly similar, albeit lagged, proportional decline in employment. Official unemployment rates increased rapidly to over 10 percent, even as a considerable part of the reduction in employment was followed by a reduction in the active labor force.[23]

For the period 1990–93, the decline in output affected most sectors and all major demand categories (Table 3.1). In the beginning, it was particularly pronounced in industry and construction, while agricultural output fell very sharply in 1992–93 as a result of severe droughts the effects of which were further aggravated by uncertainties and initial inefficiencies related to the transfer of property claims in this sector. More modest declines were recorded

---

[22]Moreover, given a persistently higher rate of consumer-over-producer price inflation, maintaining real consumption wages implies steadily increasing product wages and, with insufficient growth in productivity, until 1992, falling enterprise profits. For a more detailed discussion of these issues, see Lutz (1994b).

---

[23]See Lutz (1994b).

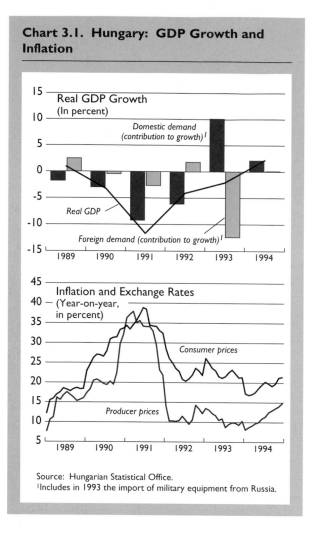

Chart 3.1. Hungary: GDP Growth and Inflation

Source: Hungarian Statistical Office.
[1]Includes in 1993 the import of military equipment from Russia.

GDP growth reflected a strong expansion of domestic demand, in particular investment but also private consumption, as households' disposable real income increased by over 3 percent.

While it seems clear that the official statistics overestimate the actual decline in output,[25] it is still generally acknowledged that a substantial decline indeed occurred.[26] It also seems likely that the decline was caused by a multitude of shocks rather than a single one. And while some of the shocks were exogenous to Hungarian policies, others probably also reflected what, in hindsight, have turned out to be home-grown policy mistakes.

The disruption of trade among the CMEA countries obliterated some of the existing productive structure and interrupted long-standing business links that could only be replaced to a limited extent by trade with other markets in the short run. And even though the importance of CMEA trade disruptions may have been less in Hungary than in several other countries—with ruble trade accounting for about 42 percent of exports toward the end of the communist era in 1988 (and an additional 10 percent was conducted in convertible currencies with the then-socialist countries), these disruptions clearly presented a major shock to the domestic economy. On the other hand, if the CMEA dissolution had been the only, or overwhelming, shock, one would have expected that external trade would also record the sharpest contraction in its aftermath. Yet this was not the case and the share of exports in GDP remained fairly stable during the years 1991–92.[27]

The Hungarian state has been slow to retreat from its dominant influence in the economy (see also Chart 3.2). The large role of the state, including through its part in income redistribution, has required a heavy tax burden with disincentives for work and investment, and negative effects on overall production in the economy. The fiscal revenue burden remained high at over 50 percent, and the

in most service sectors, reflecting an increase in some subsectors following their neglect in prior decades. Among demand categories, gross investment declined from some 26 percent of GDP in 1989 to around 15 percent in 1992, but has since regained about 6 percentage points of GDP.[24] Although the growth contribution from the external sector was overall somewhat negative during 1990–92, a sharp deterioration occurred only in 1993. At that time, a rebound in domestic demand contributed to a strong acceleration in imports while exports fell by about 12 percent in real terms, resulting in a sharp widening of the external gap. In 1994, the external balance remained broadly unchanged and the recovery of

---

[24]Probably even more than other data series, there are serious problems concerning the quality of the investment figures. In particular, they include hardly plausible large swings in stock building; the share of fixed investment in GDP, on the other hand, was much more stable and was in 1994 about 1 percentage point lower than in 1989.

[25]The overestimation is partly reflected in a lack of data coverage and the correspondingly large size of the underground economy, estimated at some 20–30 percent of official GDP. Regarding data difficulties in countries in transition, see EBRD (1994).

[26]For an early review of the experience in transforming economies, see Bruno (1992).

[27]Furthermore, the transmission mechanism related to the end of the CMEA would importantly operate through a change in relative prices (presumably even in Hungary, even though prices there were more closely aligned with world market levels than in other CMEA countries). If this were a dominant feature, one would have expected considerable variations across tradable sectors in their output developments; however, some early work on this issue seems to suggest that this was not the case, and that, on the contrary, macroeconomic (i.e., more general) shocks were the dominant feature, at least in the industrial sector (see Borensztein and Ostry (1994)).

Table 3.1. Hungary: Selected Economic Indicators

	1989	1990	1991	1992	1993	Estimate 1994
Real economy *(change in percent)*						
Real GDP	0.7	−3.5	−11.9	−4.3	−2.3	2.0
Real domestic demand[1]	−1.6	−3.1	−9.4	−6.1	7.0	2.3
Private consumption	−0.3	−3.6	−5.8	−1.3	1.4	1.3
Gross fixed investment	−5.0	−5.2	−0.6	−2.8	−0.7	11.5
Exports (real)	8.6	−5.3	−15.3	5.4	−11.9	12.1
Imports (real)[1]	1.8	−4.3	−8.8	0.5	18.6	10.2
CPI (end of year)	18.2	34.6	31.0	24.7	21.1	21.2
GDP deflator	18.4	26.0	26.0	21.7	24.2	19.4
Employment	−0.6	−0.6	−3.1	−9.6	−9.3	−1.0
Unemployment rate *(in percent of labor force)*	0.6	1.4	7.5	12.3	12.1	10.9
Public finance *(in percent of GDP)*						
Consolidated state budget balance[2]	−0.8	0.9	−4.0	−6.6	−7.5	−6.1
Excluding privatization receipts	−0.8	0.9	−4.0	−7.3	−7.5	−6.9
Public debt						
General government	...	63.3	75.9	80.8	91.1	88.4
Consolidated public sector[3]	...	56.5	67.7	66.5	84.5	82.5
Money and credit *(end of year, percent change)*						
Domestic credit	11.9	33.3	8.0	10.3	16.8	13.8
Broad money (M2)	3.5	13.8	29.4	27.3	16.8	13.6
Interest rate *(90-day treasury bills, end-December)*	...	33.7	32.4	14.7	24.3	31.8
Gross national saving[4]	25.1	27.3	17.8	14.4	9.2	12.6
Gross investment[4]	25.3	25.4	20.4	15.2	19.7	21.5
Balance of payments						
Current account[4]						
In percent of GDP	−1.9	1.2	0.9	0.9	−9.6	−9.5
In billions of U.S. dollars	−0.6	0.3	0.4	0.3	−3.5	−3.9
Reserves in convertible currencies						
National valuation of gold						
In billions of U.S. dollars	1.7	1.2	4.0	4.4	6.7	6.8
In months of merchandise imports	3.5	2.3	5.3	5.2	7.1	7.2
Gross external debt in convertible currencies						
In percent of GDP	73.2	64.6	73.3	63.4	64.4	69.5
In billions of U.S. dollars	20.4	21.3	22.7	21.4	24.5	27.7[5]
Public and publicly guaranteed debt	16.6	18.0	18.9	17.8	20.4	21.5[5]
Private creditors	14.6	15.3	15.1	14.0	16.5	17.4[5]
Bonds	3.4	4.7	6.0	6.8	10.6	12.5[5]
Short-term debt	3.3	2.9	2.2	2.3	2.0	2.2[5]
Net external debt in convertible currencies						
In percent of GDP	53.1	48.4	47.1	35.7	41.4	46.3
In billions of U.S. dollars	14.9	15.9	14.6	13.1	15.0	19.0
Debt-service ratio[6]	45.4	52.3	35.0	38.6	47.4	60.8
Exchange rate						
Nominal effective rate (1985 = 100)	66.3	58.5	51.9	49.1	47.6	43.3
Real effective rate (1985 = 100)	83.7	87.1	98.7	106.5	117.4	117.3

Sources: Ministry of Finance; National Bank of Hungary; and IMF, *International Financial Statistics*.
[1] Excludes in 1993 imports of military equipment from Russia in lieu of outstanding claims by Hungary.
[2] Includes the activities of the State Development Institution; in 1990, adjustments are made to both revenues and expenditures relating to the financing of local councils to render these comparable with later data.
[3] Consolidation of general government and central bank debt.
[4] Current account deficit is on a settlements basis and differs from the saving-investment balance, which is on a national accounts basis.
[5] End-September 1994.
[6] In percent of exports of goods and nonfactor services.

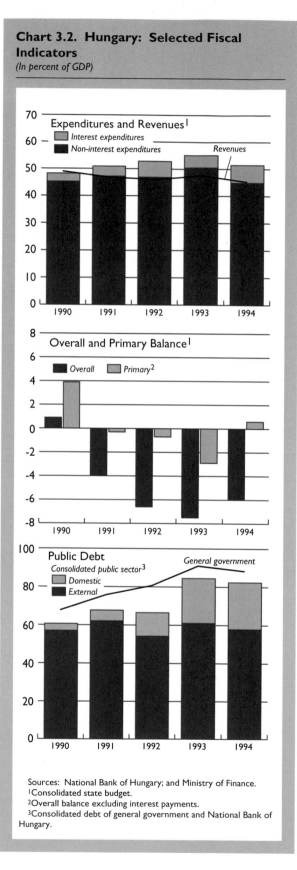

Chart 3.2. Hungary: Selected Fiscal Indicators
(In percent of GDP)

Sources: National Bank of Hungary; and Ministry of Finance.
[1]Consolidated state budget.
[2]Overall balance excluding interest payments.
[3]Consolidated debt of general government and National Bank of Hungary.

share of general government expenditure in GDP indeed increased, by almost 10 percentage points, in 1991–93 to over 60 percent. While the increase reflected in part social expenditures related to declining economic activity, adequate targeting in this and substantial cuts in other areas has not been achieved (as discussed earlier) and the state's role would appear to be too large for the development of a dynamic market-based economy. In all, inadequate progress in structural fiscal areas—including fiscal and social security reforms—has thus impeded the macroeconomic stabilization task. In addition to the level of state involvement, the widening borrowing requirement of the public sector is likely to have resulted in some crowding out of private credit, with negative effects on investment.

The effect of uncertainty on investment may have slowed the transformation process initially as enterprises postponed investment activities until at least some of the uncertainties were resolved (Dixit and Pindyck (1994)). However, in view of its political stability and the sizable inflow of foreign direct investment, this argument is probably less persuasive in Hungary for the years 1990–93 than in most other countries of Central and Eastern Europe.

Official data indicate a redistribution of income toward labor in these years, reflecting predominantly the rising burden of social security contributions. The underlying worsening of the enterprise sector became clear and was to some extent aggravated by the 1992 bankruptcy law, and enterprise losses reached nearly 15 percent of GDP in 1992. Aside from direct output effects as some enterprises entered liquidation, the deterioration in enterprise profits had negative repercussions on investment and thus on the near-term growth capacity of the economy.

A sharp rise in household saving rates at the beginning of the transformation process in 1991–92 may have weakened demand and output in this period. It seems likely that this reflected in part precautionary saving in the face of rising unemployment and general economic uncertainty. Temporarily rising real returns on financial assets after mid-1991 may also have played a role in these saving trends (Chart 3.3). The situation changed dramatically in 1993 when the share of household saving in GDP fell by about 6 percentage points.

Domestic credit growth to enterprises increased only slowly in nominal terms in 1992–93, and this may have hindered a rebound in activity (see also Calvo and Coricelli (1993)). It is likely that the slow growth of credit to enterprises in this period reflected importantly the risk assessment that priced many enterprises out of the market; aside from risks of specific enterprises, it reflected also concern about more systemic repercussions from the previously mentioned

Chart 3.3. Hungary: Selected Monetary Indicators

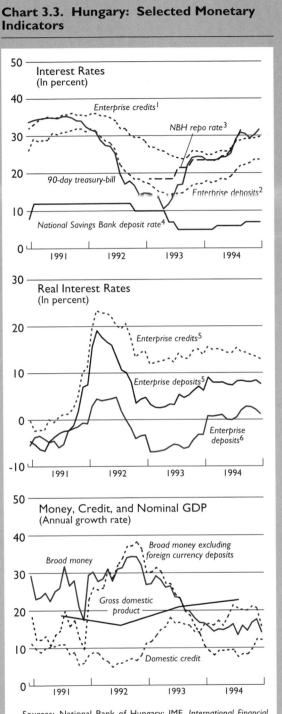

Sources: National Bank of Hungary; IMF, *International Financial Statistics*; and IMF staff estimates.

[1]Less than one-year maturity.

[2]Less than one-year, more than one-month maturity.

[3]Three-month active repo rate. Facility terminated September 5, 1994.

[4]Sight deposit rate.

[5]Deflated by the producer price index.

[6]Deflated by the consumer price index.

bankruptcy law. On the credit supply side, the financial weakness of the banking sector may also have slowed credit expansion, with much of the available credit in turn being absorbed by the public sector.

Among other factors that had a negative impact on growth in Hungary during this period were the recession in Western Europe (and the depression in other transforming economies); a prolonged drought with large output losses in the agricultural sector; and the UN sanctions against the neighboring Federal Republic of Yugoslavia (Serbia/Montenegro).

Inflation

Inflation rates accelerated in 1990–91 and peaked in mid-1991 at around 40 percent (Chart 3.1). Following a subsequent decline, consumer price inflation has shown considerable inertia and has remained stuck at around 20 percent early 1992.

The persistence of inflation reflects to some extent the gradual removal of subsidies, implemented over a number of years and indeed still ongoing. While this has limited the size of price increases at any particular time, it is likely that the cost of this policy has been an entrenchment of inflationary expectations. Moreover, it has led to a persistent gap between producer and consumer prices, amounting to some 10 percentage points for much of 1992–94, which may have aggravated distortions in the economy and complicated monetary policy.[28]

Increases in labor incomes provided a persistent cost push over this period. This reflected increases in nonwage labor costs and in-kind labor compensation, with the faster rise in the latter taking advantage of the large implicit tax differential. But even gross nominal wages for full-time employees did not show the large decrease recorded in other transforming economies. During 1990–93, real wages (nominal wages deflated by the consumer price index) fell by only about 2 percent, and the decrease was more than recovered by the 3½ percent rise in real wages in 1994.

The institutional features of the labor market, previously discussed, probably contributed to the relatively stable behavior in real wages despite the sharp contraction in output and employment. It seems that there were only weak incentives for wages to respond to these unfavorable macroeconomic conditions, due in particular to still rather soft budget constraints for some public enterprises and in the public sector more generally. Sizable

---

[28]Among other things, it has contributed to high real lending rates for enterprises (with lending rates deflated by the producer price index), even at times when the return for depositors was still negative (with deposit rates deflated by the consumer price index).

support for many workers that were laid off, including through various pension schemes, also played a role, as did the centralized bargaining institutions in Hungary where outsiders, and possibly also the private sector employers, played a relatively weak role.

The conduct of monetary policy probably contributed to persistent inflation. Without well-articulated and well-understood monetary targets, including for the exchange rate, the economy lacked a clearly visible nominal anchor. Exchange rates were adjusted intermittently in an ad hoc fashion against a basket of currencies, with considerable uncertainty surrounding each devaluation and the exchange rate path. Moreover, domestic monetary conditions also lacked at times the necessary firmness and stability for reducing inflation. This was particularly apparent in 1992 and early 1993, when an easing of monetary conditions was accompanied by a sharp decline in market rates (Chart 3.2). Subsequently, budgetary financing needs and weakening external balances led to monetary tightening; in the event, three-month treasury bill rates increased from a low of about 10 percent in April 1993 to over 30 percent by late November 1994, and some 33 percent in the first quarter of 1995. However, more frequent and at times larger step devaluations—of 7½ percent in August 1994 and 8¼ percent in March 1995—partly offset these developments and inflation rates began to rise again in the second half of 1994 (further fueled, at the beginning of 1995, by increases in the administered price of energy); by May 1995, the year-on-year increase in the consumer price index exceeded 30 percent.

The inability of monetary policy to address the inflation problem more decisively reflected to some extent insufficient support from other policy instruments, notably fiscal policy. Public sector dissaving also contributed to the large external current account gap that increasingly required the attention of monetary policy instruments, at times at the expense of a lower inflation rate. The effectiveness of monetary policy has been further hampered by the ample availability of government guaranteed and subsidized credits. This has effectively shielded a considerable segment of the market from the transmission mechanism of indirect monetary instruments through interest rates; these forms of credit amounted to about two thirds of the increase in credit to enterprises in 1994 (and about 20 percent of the total outstanding stock of enterprise credit at the end of 1994).

External Balances and Debt

In the early phase of the transformation process, the external accounts performed considerably better than anticipated. In terms of the saving-investment balance, this reflected primarily a strong improvement in household saving in 1991–92 and weak investment demand. On the trade side, Hungary was initially successful in containing imports even as the trading system was liberalized. At the same time exports were redirected to Western markets, and the share of industrial countries in total exports increased from 40 percent in 1989 to almost 70 percent in 1992.

The external current account recorded a surplus in each year during the period 1990–92, and the net debt level decreased by $800 million to about 43 percent of GDP (Table 3.2 and Chart 3.4). Moreover, Hungary attracted larger inflows of foreign direct investment than any other country in Central or Eastern Europe, averaging over $1 billion in this period. Following the renewed access to capital markets after 1990, the central bank borrowed from abroad to bolster its foreign exchange reserves.

In 1993–94, the external current account deteriorated markedly. With sharply falling exports and continued strong growth in imports, the current account moved into a deficit of over $3½ billion (close to 10 percent of GDP) in each of these years. Among the factors contributing to these developments were accumulated problems in cost competitiveness with comparatively large increases in labor costs (and profit reductions) in Hungary during 1990–92 (Chart 3.4), which left labor costs considerably above those in other transforming economies, and the strong rebound in domestic demand discussed earlier, as well as the recession in Western Europe; moreover, the large dissavings of the state—with consolidated budget deficits excluding privatization receipts of about 7 percent of GDP—weakened the macroeconomic saving-investment balance. On the supply side, a drought-related reduction in agricultural exports, repercussions from the 1992 bankruptcy law, and the effects of UN sanctions on a neighboring country also played a role in the widening external deficits.

The deterioration in the current account in 1993–94 was cushioned by non-debt and debt-creating capital inflows. Foreign direct investment was particularly strong in 1993, exceeding $2 billion and helped by the partial privatization of the telecommunication sector. In international capital markets, enterprise, and especially official borrowing, increased strongly in the period, with the latter concentrated in the bond market. This was used in part to bolster the foreign exchange reserves of the central bank, which increased to $6.7 billion at the end of 1993, with a further small increase in 1994.

The worsening of the external accounts over the past two years has resulted again in an increase in foreign debt. Net debt increased by almost $6 billion during 1993–94 to close to $19 billion at the end of

Table 3.2. Hungary: Balance of Payments in Convertible Currencies[1]
(In millions of U.S. dollars)

	1989	1990	1991	1992	1993	Estimate 1994
Trade balance	536	338	189	−50	−3,247	−3,635
Exports	6,446	6,408	9,258	10,028	8,094	7,613
Imports	−5,910	−6,070	−9,069	−10,077	−11,341	−11,248
Services (net)	−2,100	−949	−797	−486	−942	−1,185
Freight and insurance, net	210	165	−80	−117	−107	−176
Travel (net)	−349	347	560	590	441	503
Credits	738	824	1,006	1,231	1,182	1,428
Debits	−1,087	−477	−446	−640	−742	−925
Interest income (net)	−1,386	−1,451	−1,331	−1,215	−1,131	−1,286
Credits	219	233	297	419	456	661
Debits	−1,605	−1,684	−1,628	−1,635	−1,587	−1,947
Government expenditures (net)	−57	18	63	78	−17	−12
Other current payments (net)	2	302	−8	178	−128	−214
Unrequited transfers (net)	126	734	860	859	732	909
Current account	−1,438	123	252	323	−3,457	−3,911
Medium- and long-term capital	1,563	349	2,198	439	5,606	2,457
Assets (net)	32	−76	−57	−146	238	36
Liabilities (net)	1,351	88	781	−886	3,039	1,325
Disbursements	3,091	2,186	3,114	2,094	6,309	5,429
Amortizations	−1,740	−2,098	−2,333	−2,980	−3,270	−4,104
Direct capital investment	180	337	1,474	1,471	2,329	1,097
Short-term capital[2]	−44	−883	−617	5	459	960
Capital account	1,519	−534	1,581	444	6,065	3,418
Overall balance	81	−411	1,833	767	2,608	−493
Financing	−87	411	−1,833	−767	−2,608	493
Reserves (increase = −)	71	559	−2,720	−758	−2,637	656
Use of Fund credit	−158	−148	887	−8	29	−163
Purchases	66	175	963	109	79	—
Repurchases	−224	−323	−76	−118	−50	−163
Memorandum items						
Debt-service ratio *(in percent of exports of GNFS)*	45.4	52.3	35.0	38.6	47.4	60.8
Interest payments *(in percent of exports of GNFS)*	20.4	21.4	14.6	13.3	15.3	19.0
Gross debt *(in millions of U.S. dollars)*	20,390	21,270	22,658	21,438	24,560	28,521
Total reserves *(in millions of U.S. dollars)*	1,725	1,166	4,017	4,380	6,736	6,769
Foreign exchange	1,246	1,069	3,935	4,348	6,692	6,727
Total reserves *(months of imports)*	3.5	2.3	5.3	5.2	7.1	7.2
Net debt *(in millions of U.S. dollars)*	16,378	15,937	14,555	13,057	14,971	18,978
Net debt *(in percent of GDP)*	56.5	48.4	47.1	35.7	41.4	46.3
Net public debt *(in percent of GDP)*[3]	69.5	61.1	60.3	40.0	40.5	42.4
Current account *(in percent of GDP)*						
Excluding reinvested profit remittances	−5.0	0.4	0.8	0.9	−9.6	−9.5
Including reinvested profit remittances	−5.0	0.4	0.8	0.7	−9.9	−10.0

Sources: National Bank of Hungary; and national authorities' and IMF staff estimates.
[1] Excluding reinvested profit remittances.
[2] Includes net errors and omissions.
[3] Excluding banking system and nonguaranteed enterprise liabilities.

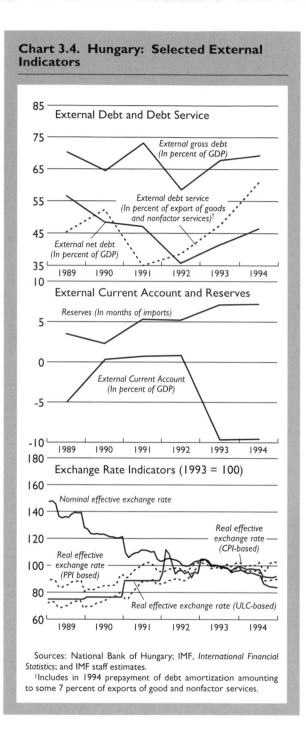

Chart 3.4. Hungary: Selected External Indicators

Sources: National Bank of Hungary; IMF, *International Financial Statistics*; and IMF staff estimates.
[1]Includes in 1994 prepayment of debt amortization amounting to some 7 percent of exports of good and nonfactor services.

1994 (above 50 percent of GDP). Gross debt surpassed $28 billion and debt-service payments were equivalent to over 50 percent of exports in 1994.[29]

[29]The actual debt-service ratio in 1994—above 60 percent—reflected in part early repayments by the central bank in order to smooth its debt-service profile.

These developments indicate an urgent need to reduce the external imbalances and initiate steps that would put the economy on a path toward lower external indebtedness—a task that is acknowledged by policymakers in Hungary who recently initiated important steps to address these issues.

Challenges and Recent Policy Response

Hungary has undertaken reforms in almost every aspect of economic activity in the past few decades, with a sharp acceleration of efforts since 1989. The task, however, is still far from completed. Macroeconomic imbalances—with large fiscal and external deficits—have emerged and domestic and external debt paths and levels require early and decisive stabilization efforts. To attain a path of high and sustainable growth, a parallel endeavor is needed to complete the sizable remaining tasks in the structural area. Indeed, the experience discussed here suggests that these two tasks are closely linked and sustained success in macroeconomic stabilization may require a more decisive pace of structural reform than Hungary has pursued in the past. The remainder of this section identifies some key outstanding structural issues and briefly describes a policy package presented by the Hungarian authorities in mid-March 1995 to address some of the stabilization and structural tasks.

The first area where structural reforms are urgently needed for both micro- and macroeconomic reasons in scale and scope is in government activities; they need to be reduced. Specifically, the level of social expenditures must be brought in line with what can be afforded. Among others things, effective pension ages will have to be raised and the contribution base broadened to place the system on a sound footing while ensuring adequate minimum pension levels. This should eventually allow for the reduction of the extremely high and distortionary social contribution rates. The size of public administration, as well as the tasks it is involved in, must also be evaluated, with a view to significantly scaling back the role of government. This can be helped by a comprehensive and timely budget information system, an area in which initial steps have begun as part of an effort to establish a centralized treasury. The latter will also improve the budgeting process, and expenditure monitoring and control.

The second area concerns the banking system. Following recapitalization, changes in incentives, and thereby in behavior, are necessary to ensure that problems do not re-emerge. This may be helped through the partial or total privatization of the banks, including potentially to foreign owners with banking experience. Moreover, the system of bank supervision needs to be substantially improved.

The third area concerns enterprise structure and governance. The new government has announced plans to reinvigorate the privatization process, including reducing the number of firms that are to remain fully or partially state owned. This should be done in a manner that is transparent and that provides firms with effective voices for capital, also in the period until privatization is completed. The latter applies particularly strongly to large state-owned, loss-making firms. It may be necessary for the Government to reintroduce direct controls over some of the actions of these firms (e.g., over wage bills) to stem their losses, and painful steps regarding their reorganization or liquidation must be undertaken.

The Hungarian Government announced in mid-March 1995 a policy package that attempts to address several of the issues raised here. Its main focus is on the immediate stabilization task, although it also contains several important structural elements. The package rests on three pillars: (1) fiscal adjustment measures that would contain the fiscal deficit excluding privatization to some 6 percent of GDP (about a 1 percentage point reduction from the similarly defined 1994 level and an over 3 percentage point correction from the deficit that would likely have occurred in the absence of measures); (2) a step devaluation of the forint by $8^{1}/_{4}$ percent against a currency basket, followed by a switch to a crawling peg exchange rate regime;[30] and (3) tighter control over wages, including in the public enterprise sector.

The fiscal measures contain several elements that would address underlying structural weaknesses. In particular, they include a switch to means testing for the various forms of family benefits and incorporate some broadening of the contribution base for social security payments (however, the implementation of these measures is subject to a review by the Constitutional Court). In the social security area, the measures would also introduce copayments for some health care benefits. In all, the package, if fully and quickly implemented, would present an important initial step in overcoming the formidable—and interrelated—stabilization and structural challenges that the Hungarian economy is currently facing.

---

[30]The rate of crawl will be 1.9 percent a month until the end of June and 1.3 percent a month for the remainder of 1995.

References

Berend, Ivan T., and Gyorgy Ránki, *The Hungarian Economy in the Twentieth Century* (London: Croom Helm, 1985).

Boote, Anthony R., and Janos Somogyi, *Economic Reform in Hungary Since 1968*, IMF Occasional Paper, No. 83 (Washington: International Monetary Fund, July 1991).

Borenzstein, Eduardo, and Jonathan Ostry, "Economic Reform and Structural Adjustment in East European Industry," IMF Working Paper, WP/94/80 (Washington: International Monetary Fund, June 1994).

Bruno, Michael, "Stabilization and Reform in Eastern Europe," *Staff Papers*, International Monetary Fund, Vol. 39 (December 1992), pp. 741–777.

Calvo, Guillermo, and Fabrizio Coricelli, "Output Collapse in Eastern Europe," *Staff Papers*, International Monetary Fund, Vol. 40 (March 1993), pp. 32–52.

Dixit, Avinash K., and Robert S. Pindyck, *Investment Under Uncertainty* (Princeton: Princeton University Press, 1994).

European Bank for Reconstruction and Development (EBRD), "Are Growth Estimates for Eastern Europe Too Pessimistic?" Appendix 11.1 in *Transition Report* (London: EBRD, October 1994).

Kopits, George, "Hungary: A Case of Gradual Fiscal Reform," in *Transition to Market: Studies in Fiscal Reform*, ed. by Vito Tanzi (Washington: International Monetary Fund, 1993).

Lutz, Mark S., "Fiscal Structure and Developments in Hungary," in *Hungary: Reform and Decentralization of the Public Sector*, Volume II, Chapter 2, Report No. 10061–HU (Washington: International Bank for Reconstruction and Development, May 1992).

———(1994a), "Fiscal Adjustment" (mimeograph, Washington: International Monetary Fund, June 1994).

———(1994b), "Recent Shifts in Labor and Capital Compensation in Hungary" (mimeograph, Washington: International Monetary Fund, October 1994).

———(1994c), "Tax Reform in Hungary" (mimeograph, Washington: International Monetary Fund, 1994).

Ministry of Finance, *Scope of Authority and Duties of the Minister of Finance*, Public Finance in Hungary, No. 25 (Budapest, 1985).

———, *Management of Public Budgetary Institutions*, Public Finance in Hungary, No. 31 (Budapest, 1986).

———, *Act on Public Finances (Unified, Up-To Date Text)*, Public Finance in Hungary, No. 42 (Budapest, 1988).

———(1991a), *Governmental Programme of Conversion and Development for the Hungarian Economy (Stabilization and Convertibility)*, Public Finance in Hungary, No. 82, Vol. I (Budapest, 1991).

———(1991b), *Programme of Action and Economic Legislation*, Public Finance in Hungary, No. 82, Vol. II (Budapest, 1991).

———(1991c), *Act on Compensation*, Public Finance in Hungary, No. 84 (Budapest, 1991).

———(1991d), *New Act on Accounting*, Public Finance in Hungary, No. 86 (Budapest, 1991).

———(1992a), *Act on the National Bank of Hungary*, Public Finance in Hungary, No. 88 (Budapest, 1992).

———(1992b), *Act on the Investment Fund*, Public Finance in Hungary, No. 89 (Budapest, 1992).

———(1992c), *Act on Financial Institutions*, Public Finance in Hungary, No. 91 (Budapest, 1992).

———(1992d), *Act on Employees' Stock Ownership Programme*, Public Finance in Hungary, No. 104 (Budapest, 1992).

———(1992e), *Different Acts on Compensation*, Public Finance in Hungary, No. 107 (Budapest, 1992).

———, *Act on National Deposit Insurance Fund*, Public Finance in Hungary, No. 121 (Budapest, 1993).

Morgan, J.P., "Hungary: Forint Debt Securities," October 1993.

National Bank of Hungary, "The Law on the Central Bank," *Market Letter*, No. 10–11 (Budapest, 1991).

Plant, Roger, "Labor Standards and Structural Adjustments in Hungary," International Labor Office Occasional Paper, No. 7 (Geneva, April 1993).

IV   Stabilization and Structural Change in Russia, 1992–94

Vincent Koen and Michael Marrese

The public perception of Russia's economic transition is that the old system has been successfully destroyed but that it has not yet been replaced by a sustainable democracy and an effective market economy. Following decades of central planning and systematic repression of market forces under the Soviet regime, the relatively peaceful dismantling of the old order has been a major achievement. However, Russia has not yet implemented the full complement of economic policies needed to solidify a market system.

This paper develops three ideas. First, the quest for macroeconomic stabilization since 1992 has been characterized by ups and downs rather than continuous improvement. Nevertheless, it is possible to identify some underlying trends in output, inflation, and financial policies. Second, conventional macroeconomic wisdom is more relevant for Russia than acknowledged by those who dismiss it with the argument that "Russia is unique." Third, Russia is undergoing a structural metamorphosis: the former key dichotomies (such as heavy versus light industry, or even state versus private enterprises) are superseded by new ones (in particular, "survivalist" versus "subsidized" enterprises).

The focus is on the significant structural progress that has occurred despite persistent macroeconomic instability (large financial imbalances, continuing high inflation, and exchange rate crises). Not discussed in this paper, notwithstanding their obvious importance, are the international community's assistance to Russia,[1] external developments in general,[2] and the lessons that can be drawn from the experiences of all those countries that were once part of the Soviet Union.[3]

One rule of thumb for nonresidents trying to evaluate what is actually happening in Russia is that "[i]n times of trouble, reality is never as bad as it seems, and when circumstances look auspicious, reality is never as good as it seems."[4] Keeping this warning in mind, major occurrences over the past few years are categorized either as underlying trends that capture the essence of Russia's transformation or as disruptions that, although newsworthy and often quite serious, can be described ex post as transitory. Trends, however, can only be identified in light of the constraints and opportunities faced by policymakers in Russia at the onset of the transition.

Background

The conditions under which virtually every formerly planned economy started its transition were in many ways quite discouraging. Common problems included the dismantling of the Council for Mutual Economic Assistance (CMEA), the sudden dissolution of the Soviet Union, a West European recession, the absence of a market-oriented infrastructure, obsolete capital stocks, and very limited integration into the world economy. At the same time, one can argue that these countries were ripe for development because their workforces were highly educated and wages would be relatively low.

For a number of reasons, however, it was likely that the transition would be more difficult for Russia than for many of the countries in Central and Eastern Europe:

- The sudden dissolution of the U.S.S.R. disrupted trade and payments arrangements among the newly emerging states and provided Russia with

Note: In addition to thanking the discussants mentioned in the preface, the authors gratefully acknowledge useful comments by John Odling-Smee and Thomas Wolf.

[1]Brau (1994) and Hernández-Catá (1995) discuss the role of the IMF.

[2]On this topic, see Christensen (1994), IMF (1994a) and Koen and Meyermans (1994).

[3]Odling-Smee and Wolf (1994) address this issue.

[4]Looking at Russia in the early 1920s, Keynes (1925, pp. 18–19) noted that "the economic system of Soviet Russia has undergone and is undergoing such rapid changes that it is impossible to obtain a precise and accurate account of it. . . . Almost everything one can say about the country is true and false at the same time."

a monetary system that was not completely under its control.[5]

- The Soviet Union's enormous size, the political vacuum left by its sudden breakup and the subsequent demise of the Communist Party left regions with administrative infrastructures that were both independent from and suspicious of Moscow. The vastness of the Soviet Union had necessitated the creation of regional bureaucracies, which duplicated national governmental and legislative bodies. Since late 1991, these regional bodies increasingly served as competing seats of authority responding skeptically to Moscow's leadership, not least because of the decades of poor decisions imposed by the center.

- Russia inherited the 1977 Soviet Constitution, which considerably weakened the federal government's control over the economy. In particular, the Constitution did not define the respective roles of the legislative and executive branches of the federal government, opening the way for a power struggle between the two. Moreover, it gave Russia's 16 autonomous republics many of the economic rights of an independent country at a time when the center and the regions had not yet agreed on how to share tax revenues and apportion expenditure responsibilities.[6]

- Russia had been more completely isolated from the West than most countries of Central and Eastern Europe (though perhaps not as much as other states of the former Soviet Union, the Baltic states, Bulgaria, or Albania). Russia's legal and financial infrastructures were therefore decidedly nonmarket, and Russian businesses were far less integrated into the world economy than their Central and Eastern Europe counterparts.[7]

- Russia faced the enormous fiscal burden of undoing a military industrial structure and a network of enterprises that had been created based on strategic rather than economic considerations. Soviet militarization combined with reliance on increasingly ineffective increases of factor inputs had saddled Russia with heavy industry and agriculture, which in late 1991 were both disproportionately large and highly inefficient. At the same time, light industry and services were vastly underdeveloped. Russia inherited two additional costly idiosyncrasies: the Northern Territories, which comprise two thirds of the country's land area but only 7.5 percent of its population, and hundreds of single-enterprise towns, which had been created for reasons of national security.

- Beginning with the Gorbachev era, large budget deficits have been a major structural problem. The antialcoholism campaign started in 1985 caused substantial losses in indirect tax revenue. Later, the Law on State Enterprises of 1987 allowed firms to retain a higher share of internally generated funds and to allocate retained resources more freely among wages, investment, bonuses, and social-cultural benefits. In effect, the federal government's share of national income had been reduced without a concomitant cut in the federal government's expenditure responsibilities.[8]

- The political and economic liberalization that took place in the Soviet Union from the mid-1980s onward was not accompanied by market-oriented institution building. As a result, the center was stripped of much of its control over enterprises. This combination made it easier for corruption to grow rapidly and for criminal elements to gain control over many enterprises.[9]

- In late 1991, no broad consensus about a transition strategy existed, even among reformers, who themselves held only isolated positions within the Government and the central bank. This meant that reformers had little control over the administrative apparatus. At the same time, no major interest groups were committed to macroeconomic stabilization.

Yet Russia at the beginning of 1992 enjoyed advantages most other transition economies lacked: (1) vast mineral resources; (2) a huge internal market; (3) the scope for significant terms of trade gains vis-à-vis the other countries of the former Soviet Union and the Baltic states as export prices for energy carriers were raised toward world market levels;[10] (4) sectors in which there was enormous potential for improving efficiency (agriculture and energy); (5) the attention of the West; and (6) the virtual absence of a "restitution" problem. Moreover, it ought to be noted that starting conditions were also dismal in the Baltics and in Albania, yet

---

[5]See Odling-Smee and Lorie (1993) and IMF (1994a).

[6]Open conflicts did not surface earlier because the Constitution was ignored in practice and the hierarchically organized Communist Party was the dominant authority.

[7]In particular, the payments system inherited by the countries of the former Soviet Union and the Baltic states was poorly suited to enacting payments among increasingly market-oriented enterprises.

[8]See IMF and others (1991) and Vavilov and Vyugin (1991).
[9]See Grossman (1993).
[10]See the estimates presented in IMF (1994a).

did not prevent stabilization from taking hold in these countries.

Trends

Russia has not undergone "economic shock therapy," even though the Russian people have endured the shock of the price liberalization of January 1992 and tumultuous political struggles between the executive and legislative branches of the federal government and between the center and regions. Instead, Russia's transition has been an experiment in economic gradualism and massive political realignment. Budget constraints have been imposed by the authorities only gradually through the deliberate reduction of financial transfers to enterprises, sequestration of budgetary expenditures, and structural reforms. As a result, many enterprises have been left with no viable alternative than to restructure. A new constitution clarifying the respective responsibilities of the branches of the federal government was adopted in December 1993.

The output collapse had already begun by 1990, when the energy sector was plagued with distribution problems, strikes and parts shortages, and trade with Eastern Europe was disrupted. The decline became a major recession in 1991 with the dismantling of the CMEA, political uncertainty, and the announced breakup of the Soviet Union. Further steep drops in officially measured real GDP followed in each of the next three years (Table 4.1). In the autumn of 1994, the Russian authorities were projecting a further large fall in year-on-year real GDP for 1995, which was not inconsistent with data indicating that industrial output began to rise in the fourth quarter of 1994 (Chart 4.1).[11]

Even though output most likely fell by less than the 50-odd percent cumulative drop recorded thus far in official GDP statistics, the magnitude of the decline has exceeded the depth of any depression in Russia during the previous seventy years and may have been on the same order as the contraction of close to one third observed in the United States between 1929 and 1933.[12] The length and severity of the output collapse has been induced by the complex interaction of (1) the actual demise of the Union itself and the consequent disruption of trade links due in part to inadequate payments and settlement systems among the newly independent coun-

tries, and in part to deliberate decisions to lessen dependence on traditional suppliers and customers; (2) sharp cutbacks in investment, defense spending, and, eventually, financial transfers from the central authorities to enterprises; (3) the increase in relative energy prices that made many enterprises unprofitable; (4) an upsurge in foreign competition stemming from increased openness of the economy and substantial real appreciation of the exchange rate during the second half of 1993; and (5) the failure to achieve macroeconomic stability at an early stage in the transformation.[13]

Since 1989, when overall production in Russia officially peaked, the output statistics depict unrelenting gloom; yet there has not been widespread, sustained social upheaval. One explanation could be that living standards have not suffered anywhere near as much as the loss in measured output would indicate. Indeed, in contrast to the prolonged and sharp drop in measured output, household consumption proved more resilient. Taking into account estimates for street and informal trade, retail sales declined only marginally in 1991 and 1992 and have been rising anew since 1993. Similarly, real wages have declined much less since mid-1992 than gross industrial output (Chart 4.1).[14]

The freeing of prices announced in late 1991 and enacted in January 1992 resulted in an almost 300 percent price surge, which far surpassed the jumps associated with large-scale price liberalization in Central and Eastern Europe.[15] Subsequent monthly inflation came down to the high single digits by mid-1992, picked up to 25 percent or more from September through February 1993, then through October 1993 averaged about 20 percent (Chart 4.1). In the fall of 1993, the process of disinflation began to take hold when the Ministry of Finance resorted to sequestration to avoid hyperinflation (see below), and inflation averaged 14 percent over the winter.[16] Continued reliance on sequestration drove average inflation down under 7 percent a month from March

---

[11]The monthly Goskomstat industrial production series should be interpreted with caution because it was redefined from July 1994 to include an estimate of the production of small enterprises.

[12]See Gavrilenkov and Koen (1994). Officially measured cumulative drops in real GDP were about 20 percent in Poland and the Czech Republic, 25 percent in the Slovak Republic, 30 percent in Romania and Estonia, 40 percent in Bulgaria and Albania, and 50 percent in Latvia and Lithuania.

[13]See IMF (1992), (1993), and (1995a) and World Bank (1992) for details on the evolution of output, employment, real wages, and living standards.

[14]This consumption-production paradox occurred in most transition economies, as the state sector that was integrated into the statistical system withered away while small and medium-sized enterprises with inadequate statistical coverage grew rapidly (see, e.g., Berg (1994) on Poland).

[15]About 80 percent of wholesale and 90 percent of retail prices were freed (in value terms, at 1991 relative prices). However, price controls were still in effect for many basic goods and services, and the state distribution sector was constrained by a ceiling on its markup ratio. See Koen and Phillips (1993) for details.

[16]Until the end of 1993, when the new constitution was adopted and the formula-based system of fiscal federalism was soon to be introduced, inflation was fueled by the Presidency's and the Parliament's attempts to buy regional political support. Since then, such competition has lessened.

Table 4.1. Russia: Summary Indicators
(Year averages unless specified otherwise)

	1991	1992	1993	1994[1]
Macroeconomic indicators				
Real GDP *(percent change)*[2]	−13	−19	−12	−15
CPI *(within-year percent change)*[3]	144	2,318	840	215
Real wage (1987 = 100)[4,5,6]	119	86	90	83
Real ruble M2 *(within-year percent change)*[6]	−19	−75	−43	−4
Enlarged government deficit *(percent of GDP)*[7]	16	21	7	9
Unbudgeted federal import subsidies	...	12	2	0
Seignorage *(percent of GDP)*[5,8]	...	26	12	6
Velocity of ruble broad money *(end-year)*[9]	1.6	6.4	10.5	10.9
Exchange rate against U.S. dollar[5,10]				
Nominal	...	222	933	2,205
Real (July 1992 = 100, rise denotes appreciation)[6]	...	75	156	282
Monthly real interest rate *(end-year)*[11]	−11	−15	4	−2
Dollarization ratio *(end-year, in percent)*[12]	17	41	29	29
Structural indicators				
Privatization *(flow of firms privatized, thousands)*	1	47	43	22
Share of private sector in recorded retail trade *(in percent)*	24	35	53	66
Privatized portion of apartments *(end-year, in percent)*[13]	0.5	8	25	32
Number of private farms *(end-year, thousands)*	49	183	270	279
Availability of foodstuffs *(end-year, in percent)*[14]	28	54	72	91
Domestic price of crude oil *(end-year, in percent of world price)*	...	20–25	40–45	30–35

Sources: National authorities; IMF, *International Financial Statistics*; and authors' calculations.
[1]Preliminary estimates.
[2]Official Goskomstat estimates.
[3]Urban CPI for 1991–92, expanded CPI for 1993–94.
[4]Abstracting from wage arrears.
[5]Average of monthlies.
[6]Using the CPI as a deflator.
[7]Federal and local governments, plus extrabudgetary funds, plus unbudgeted import subsidies; average of quarterly ratios to GDP. For 1991, annual notional budget deficit (IMF 1992) over annual GDP.
[8]Change in base money divided by GDP. The 1992 estimate is for June to December only.
[9]Annualized December GDP divided by end-December ruble M2.
[10]Rate quoted on Moscow interbank currency exchange.
[11]End-year CBR refinance rate deflated by December CPI inflation.
[12]Foreign exchange deposits with domestic banks over total M2 (since foreign exchange holdings in the form of cash or deposits abroad are excluded, this measure is downward biased).
[13]Measured by the number of apartments.
[14]Average proportion of main cities where items were available in state stores.

through September 1994. However, failure to control the fiscal deficit in the third quarter produced the expected upsurge in prices, and monthly inflation exceeded 15 percent by late 1994. Preliminary evidence since then indicates that inflation once again began to move downward.

Along with the very gradual decline in inflation, the actual and perceived net costs of inflation have climbed steadily. Actual costs escalated especially sharply in 1992 when inflation caused a flight from domestic money, with real ruble M2 plummeting and dollarization surging. The lack of confidence in the ruble contributed to capital flight—thus adding to the investment slump—and had adverse distri-

butional consequences.[17] In 1993, real ruble M2 continued to decline rapidly, although dollarization was reversed in tandem with the over 200 percent within-year real appreciation of the ruble against the U.S. dollar. In 1994, real ruble M2 dipped modestly and no further dollarization was recorded. However, the main benefit of inflation, namely inflation tax receipts as measured by seigniorage, fell by roughly one half (Table 4.1). Perceptions that inflation is detrimental to growth have gradually become more widespread because the authorities as well as

---

[17]See Easterly and Vieira da Cunha (1994).

Chart 4.1. Russia: Selected Macroeconomic Indicators

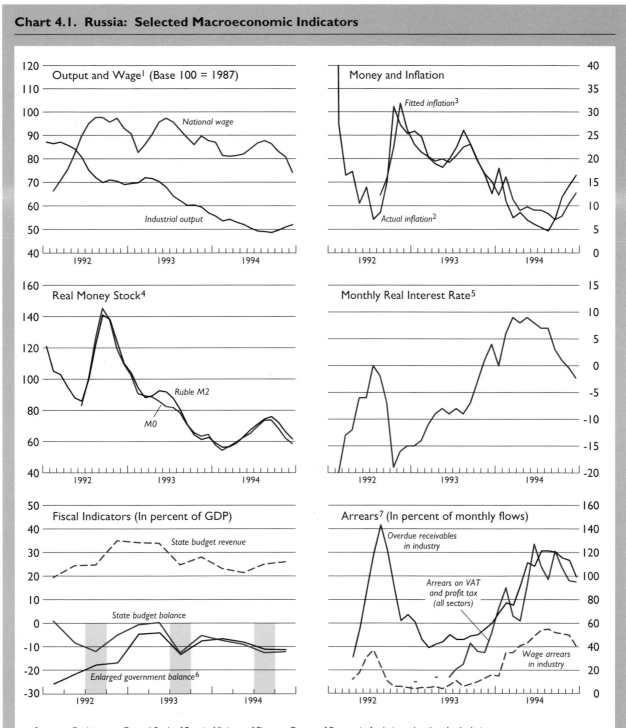

Sources: Goskomstat; Central Bank of Russia; Ministry of Finance; Center of Economic Analysis; and authors' calculations.

[1]Three-month moving average of deseasonalized real industrial output and of economy-wide average real wage abstracting from wage arrears (using the CPI as a deflator).

[2]Monthly increase in the CPI, in percent (urban CPI in 1992, expanded CPI thereafter).

[3]Based on equation (1) in the text.

[4]Using the CPI as a deflator; July 1992 = 100. M0 includes banks' correspondent accounts with the CBR.

[5]Average monthly CBR refinance rate deflated by contemporaneous CPI inflation.

[6]Enlarged government includes state budget (federal plus local), extrabudgetary funds, and unbudgeted import subsidies.

[7]Flows used to deflate nominal arrears stocks: wage bill, value of production, and VAT and profit tax receipts.

economic agents not only have endured the negative features of inflation, but also have come to recognize the contribution of macroeconomic stability to the economic turnaround in Poland, Hungary, the Czech Republic, the Slovak Republic, and the Baltic countries.

Enterprises have generally been slow in adapting to changing market conditions, as illustrated by the magnitude of subsidies, the size of directed credits extended on a nonmarket basis by the Central Bank of Russia (CBR) and the Ministry of Finance, and the accumulation of interenterprise arrears. However, macroeconomic evidence, on the whole, points to a gradual hardening of budget constraints for Russian enterprises.[18]

Subsidies from federal and local budgets declined from 14 percent of GDP in 1992 to 7 percent in 1993 and fell further in 1994, while unbudgeted import subsidies from the federal government fell from 12 percent of GDP in 1992 to 2 percent in 1993, and essentially disappeared in 1994.[19] Directed credit—a form of quasi-fiscal spending—has fallen sharply, from 48 percent of banking system credit to the rest of the economy in 1992, to 29 and 23 percent in 1993 and 1994, respectively.[20] The sharp increase in real interest rates during 1993 (Chart 4.1) further contributed to harden budget constraints, though real interest rates fluctuated widely in 1994—actually becoming negative by the end of 1994. However, and partly as a response, the arrears problem has reappeared (Chart 4.1): by late 1994, and deflated by the relevant flows, recorded overdue receivables in industry approached the levels that ignited the central bank rescue of enterprises holding such receivables during the second half of 1992, while wage arrears in industry and tax arrears in general stood at record highs.

Tax revenues collected by the federal and local governments hovered around 29 percent of GDP in 1992 and 1993, but fell to 24 percent of GDP in 1994. These annual figures, however, mask two divergent trends. From the second quarter of 1992 through mid-1993, revenue rose as new taxes were introduced and as enterprises benefited from financial transfers from the Government and the CBR.[21] Later, as these transfers were reduced and notwithstanding the reverse Tanzi effect, and as in some cases tax exemptions replaced straight subsidies, tax revenues displayed a downward trend and tax arrears an upward trend (Chart 4.1).[22]

One response to the decline in revenue has been the cutback in expenditure, with the share of federal and local government expenditures in GDP falling from 44 percent in 1992, to 38 percent in 1993, and to 36 percent in 1994. The Ministry of Finance has also sought seemingly innovative ways to finance the federal budget, clear government arrears, and solve the problem of interenterprise arrears. These initiatives, however, have tended to delay dealing with the underlying fiscal imbalance, and have complicated the measurement of liquidity in the economy. One failed effort was the proposal floated in early 1994 to permit some commercial banks to buy government securities bearing below-market interest rates, then allow these securities to fulfill reserve requirements at the CBR (for which no interest has been paid). The CBR resisted the initiative, recognizing that such a policy would unduly favor the limited number of banks involved and would compromise monetary control. Another scheme, designed to clear the Ministry's own arrears, was implemented starting in August 1994 and has featured the issuance of a substantial volume of Ministry of Finance promissory notes (so-called KOs) at interest rates far below market levels and with a maturity of up to 90 days. Some government contractors (especially in the defense sector) were given the choice of accepting these notes or waiting for the government to pay its bills. Holders (whether the original recipients or those to whom the notes have been traded) can use them immediately to pay back taxes or can cash them in upon maturity.

On the monetary side, monthly ruble broad money growth rates have been on a bumpy downward trend, averaging 10 percent during the first half of 1992, 23 percent in the second half of 1992, 14 percent in the first quarter of 1993, 19 percent for the next five months, and 10 percent from the end of August 1993 through the end of 1994. Monetary control in 1992 and through mid-1993 was hampered by noncash credit emission by the central banks of other states of the former Soviet Union and the Baltic countries and the return of cash rubles sent to those countries. This

---

[18]Budget constraints also hardened for households: as subsidies were curtailed, the relative price of services (compared with the overall CPI) rose eightfold during 1992–94.

[19]Federal import subsidies arose when imported goods financed with tied credits were resold to regions and enterprises at prices below their market value and declined as tied foreign credits dried up, see IMF (1995a).

[20]See IMF (1995a) for the 1992 and 1993 estimates. The 1994 estimate is based on preliminary monetary and fiscal data. Banking system credit to the rest of the economy includes CBR and budgetary credit to enterprises and public organizations, and loans denominated in rubles and foreign currency.

[21]As emphasized by Tanzi (1993), the distinction between fiscal and monetary policy can be blurred. For example, the 1992 injection of CBR directed credit to unwind interenterprise arrears led to a fourth-quarter increase in VAT receipts. CBR directed credits in 1992 were extended with implicit interest rate subsidies, while in 1994 explicit interest rate subsidies appeared in the budget.

[22]Tax revenue erosion has been commonplace in transition economies, caused, inter alia, by widespread tax evasion. See IMF (1995b).

became less of a problem, however, as the CBR restricted credit to other central banks of the former Soviet Union in mid-1992, as this credit was replaced by smaller amounts of intergovernmental loans in early 1993, and as pre-1993 rubles were demonetized in July 1993 (see below).[23]

Base money (defined as currency outside the CBR plus required reserves plus commercial banks' correspondent accounts at the CBR) declined sharply in real terms starting in the summer of 1992 (Chart 4.1), and the scope for seigniorage revenue shrank accordingly. The narrowing of the base for the inflation tax and the embryonic nature of the long-term government securities market imply that a fiscal deficit-GDP ratio that may not be perceived as an immediate inflationary threat in industrial countries could propel the Russian economy into hyperinflation.[24]

Disruptions

Since January 1992, the ups and downs in monetary and fiscal policy have determined the swings in monthly inflation in a fairly predictable manner. They also mirrored political struggles and searches for scapegoats, revealing the weak positions of those who fought for macroeconomic stabilization. A portion of these ups and downs is attributable to seasonality. In particular, expenditures of the federal and local governments have always been high during the third quarter (Chart 4.1). Partly related to fiscal seasonality, money growth typically picks up around the middle of the year.

Interenterprise arrears rose whenever both monetary and fiscal policy were tightened. For instance, during the first half of 1992, when the Government reduced subsidies to enterprises and consumers and cut public investment and defense spending, while the CBR restricted monetary growth, interenterprise arrears rocketed upwards as enterprises continued to ship goods to nonpaying customers, mostly in the belief that the central authorities would ultimately alleviate the problem. In turn, the accumulation of arrears lessened the effectiveness of credit and monetary policy and lowered revenue collected from the VAT and profit taxes.

Amid these circumstances, many reformers did not last long in positions of power as scapegoats were needed whenever macroeconomic policy was beginning to bite.[25] As a result, Russia had six min-

isters of finance and three central bank heads from the beginning of 1992 to the end of 1994. Several incidents come to mind. First, in July 1992, the Supreme Soviet replaced CBR Chairman Matiukhin with Mr. Gerashchenko, who at that time made it clear that he was more concerned with keeping factories operating than with fighting inflation. A deluge of subsidies and financial transfers from both the CBR and the Ministry of Finance to the regions and to the other central banks of the former Soviet Union and the Baltic countries followed. Simultaneously, the CBR addressed the arrears problem by conducting a netting out operation and providing credit to net lenders. This increased the likelihood that the arrears problem would reappear, as indeed it did in 1994.

Second, in December 1992, when the country was on the verge of hyperinflation, the Supreme Soviet caused the ouster of Acting Prime Minister Gaidar—considered the architect of Russia's economic reform effort—by refusing to confirm his appointment as prime minister. Market-oriented reform was not, however, left without a highly vocal economic spokesperson when shortly thereafter Mr. Fedorov was appointed Minister of Finance.

Third, while the deficit of the state budget (federal and local budgets) during the first half of 1993 was roughly in balance, the Government increased budgetary expenditures during the third quarter to finance the agricultural sector, Roskhleboprodukt (the state grain procurer), and the Northern Territories, in response to seasonal pressures and to political lobbying from regional leaders prior to the constitutional referendum and the December parliamentary elections. The reformers in the Government reacted by turning to the only anti-inflation policy under their control—sequestration (refusal to spend to the authorized limit). While sequestration in general is neither a sustainable nor a desirable policy option, it was justified to some extent in Russia by the then-existing jurisdictional confusion between the legislative and executive branches of government.[26] However, being forced to deal with Russia's problems in such a haphazard manner represented another setback and was followed by the departure from the government of Deputy Prime Minister in charge of Economy Gaidar and Minister of Finance Fedorov. Sequestration became even more attractive to the Ministry of Finance in 1994 because of the drop in tax revenues. In addition, the Duma did not approve the budget until June 1994, which provided the Government with some extra leeway during the first half of the year in implementing its policies.

As mentioned above, the CBR finally managed to shield Russia from inflows of cash rubles that earlier

---

[23]See Wolf (1994).

[24]In 1992, the general government deficit amounted to 10 percent of GDP in Italy, but the ratio of base money to annual GDP stood at 15 percent. In Russia, base money over annualized GDP fell from 6 percent in December 1992 to $4^{1}/_{2}$ percent in December 1994, and is likely to drop further, ceteris paribus, as settlement systems improve.

[25]See Hernández-Catá (1995).

[26]Nagy (1995) argues that in this context promises were made at all levels of government that, if fulfilled, would have promptly triggered hyperinflation.

had been issued to other countries of the former Soviet Union and the Baltic. However, the monetary reform that was carried out actually accelerated the migration of rubles into Russia and put downward pressure on the exchange rate. On Saturday July 24, 1993, the CBR unexpectedly announced that all pre-1993 bank notes would be shortly demonetized. Enterprises were given two days to transfer old notes to bank accounts, while residents received a bit more time to make the conversion. There is no final record on how many old rubles flooded into Russia during August 1993, but the upward blip in inflation of 3–4 percentage points in that month suggests it was a sizable amount. By the end of the year, and with the exception of Tajikistan, all the countries that in July 1993 were still allowing rubles to be used as legal tender had stopped doing so, and those that did not have their own national currency had introduced one.

The aforementioned political and economic disruptions twice triggered a short-lived but acute exchange rate crisis. In September 1993, following the dissolution of the Supreme Soviet by President Yeltsin, and despite heavy CBR dollar sales, the ruble depreciated by 20 percent within a couple of days (in U.S. dollar per ruble terms). On "Black Tuesday," October 11, 1994, the exchange rate plunged by 22 percent. In both cases, it subsequently recovered most of the lost ground, partly thanks to an increase in the CBR refinance rate. In both cases as well, short-run inflation expectations worsened considerably.[27]

Money, Prices, and Output

When he was last Minister of Finance, Mr. Fedorov reportedly offered Prime Minister Chernomyrdin a compilation of the work of G. Ya. Sokolnikov (author of the 1922–24 monetary reform), highlighting the latter's claim that "emission is the opium of the national economy."[28] This section revisits the issue of the impact of money creation on prices and output, and reaches a similar conclusion.

Is Inflation Essentially a Monetary Phenomenon?

In the early months following the January 1992 price liberalization, many in Russia—including numerous economic policymakers—argued that inflation was not essentially a monetary phenomenon, but rather was to be largely blamed on monopolistic behavior or other market imperfections. Over time, however, the notion that money creation is the ultimate cause of inflation has tended to become more widely accepted.[29]

Supporting evidence initially appeared in the form of simple correlations between money growth and inflation three or four months later.[30] In general, money affects prices with long and variable lags, and the length of the latter tends to fall as inflation rises. Moreover, a number of short-run shocks (such as administrative price adjustments, exchange rate swings, or discrete income policy decisions) may render the lag structure unstable. Therefore, it is perhaps not surprising that the aforementioned tight bivariate relationship broke down during 1993.

The available number of observations by now permits a re-examination of the link between money and prices using a somewhat more sophisticated lag structure.[31] The specification shown below is a five Almon lag equation based on a third-order polynomial, estimated with a first-order autoregressive Cochrane-Orcutt correction. The sum of the coefficients is constrained to one.[32] Using ruble broad money (ruble M2) as the independent variable M and consumer prices as the dependent variable P, the following result obtained, where "hats" denote the percentage change operator and t-statistics are indicated in parentheses (see also Chart 4.1):

$$\hat{P} = 0.14\hat{M} + 0.18\hat{M}_{-1} + 0.21\hat{M}_{-2} + 0.22\hat{M}_{-3}$$
$$(1.16) \quad (2.47) \quad (3.15) \quad (3.61)$$
$$+ 0.18\hat{M}_{-4} + 0.06\hat{M}_{-5} + 2.59, \quad (1)$$
$$(2.55) \quad (0.61) \quad (0.99)$$

---

[27]On two other occasions, both in connection with the exit of reformers from the Government (January 1993 and January 1994), the ruble suffered similarly large and abrupt slides, but no significant appreciation followed.

[28]The stenographer's notes of Sokolnikov's March 1922 statements to the 11th Congress of the Russian Communist Party include the following:

If a man goes to a doctor and insists that the latter give him opium, or a pain-killing injection of morphine, etc., then naturally, if the patient is near death and wants a few hours of relief from his death agonies, the doctor must give the morphine injection; any humane doctor would do that. But are we in such a position and, consequently, can we . . . institutionalize a financial policy consisting of further poisoning the organism of our economy? . . . On a wall near the Iverskaya Chapel it is written "Religion is the opium of the people"; I would like to propose that near the Supreme Soviet of the National Economy we hang a sign saying "Emission is the opium of the national economy" (Sokolnikov, 1991, p. 11), (authors' translation).

[29]But it is not unanimously shared. See for instance Petrakov (1994), who maintains that inflation in Russia is fundamentally caused by the "structural deformities" of the economy.

[30]See for example IMF (1993) or Fischer (1994).

[31]Monthly data from January 1992 through December 1994 are available for the consumer price index and the money stock. Raw money stock figures apply to the last day of each month and are converted by linear interpolation into monthly averages so as to ensure that the time frame is the same for money and prices.

[32]Such a functional form is, of course, very restrictive, but it is only meant to establish the causal relationship between money and prices, not to provide a full explanation of monthly inflation movements. An alternative approach left for future research would involve cointegration analysis (for which longer time series would be desirable).

where

$\bar{R}^2 = 0.76$,

standard error of regression = 3.73,

Durbin-Watson = 1.76,

$F(4,24) = 22.9$,

$\varepsilon = 0.71\varepsilon_{-1}$.

(4.48)

Experimentation with specifications including 4 lags or more than 5 lags, with the imposition of a constraint on the far end of the coefficients of the Almon polynomial, and with the exclusion of a constant term, did not produce substantially different results. In all cases, most of the impact of money growth on inflation was felt two, three, and four months later. Contemporaneous money was weakly significant or insignificant, while the coefficient associated with the first lag was typically relatively small and not systematically significant. Furthermore, January inflation was underpredicted in all specifications, presumably owing to the effect of the administrative price increases that are typically implemented at the beginning of the year. Finally, all equations tended to overpredict inflation in much of 1994.

Similar regressions were run replacing ruble broad money by (1) broader monetary aggregates (ruble M2 plus arrears, M2, M2 plus arrears);[33] (2) narrower ones (cash in circulation, base money); and (3) a measure of credit (net domestic assets of the banking system). In all cases, the coefficient associated with the fifth lag was not significantly different from zero at the 5 percent level of significance. The coefficient pertaining to contemporaneous money or credit was insignificant in all but one case.[34] Again, inflation in 1994 was typically overpredicted.

The implicit early presumption that prices lagged money by about one quarter is thus broadly validated. The fact that across specifications actual inflation in much of 1994 was unambiguously lower than forecast could be ascribed to a perception during the first half of the year, fostered by very high real interest rates, that disinflation was actually taking hold. Another reason could be that the recovery in actual (as opposed to officially measured) output started around early 1994. In both cases, real money demand would be expected to pick up, as it did (see the turnaround in real ruble M2 in

Chart 4.1). It should also be noted, however, that by the fall of 1994, and as real interest rates were rapidly coming down, inflation was catching up with past money growth (Chart 4.1).

Is There a Trade-Off Between Output and Disinflation?

The domestic debate on stabilization in Russia initially placed a heavy focus on what some perceived as a trade-off between output and disinflation. In 1992 and 1993, however, neighboring countries (particularly Ukraine) experiencing much higher inflation witnessed output declines on the same order of magnitude as Russia, while other countries of the former Soviet Union (particularly the Baltic states) successfully brought down inflation and saw an early turnaround in output. As a result, the claim that there was a trade-off increasingly lost credibility. Broader cross-country evidence confirms that in the long run, indulging in more inflation if anything is detrimental to output growth.[35]

The issue resurfaced in early 1994, however, as measured output collapsed further and disinflation materialized. Some then argued that there might at least be a short run trade-off, insofar as a genuine financial squeeze would immediately cause loss-making enterprises to stop producing but would only spur growth of the profitable ones over time. It was also pointed out that in the context of an underdeveloped financial market, a credit crunch could hurt firms that are viable but unable to borrow. On the other hand, the deeper the transformation-induced fall in output, the stronger is the pressure for inflationary subsidies to ailing firms.[36] On that account, one could expect a negative correlation between output and inflation.

To try and test these hypotheses, a large number of regressions of output on various measures of money, credit, prices and interest rates, and lags thereof were run. In the absence of a reasonably plausible monthly real GDP series, output was measured by deseasonalized gross industrial output. Output was introduced both in level terms and as a deviation from trend, with the trend defined in several ways.

In stark contrast to the regressions of prices on money, no consistent and robust results emerged. While some specifications showed a significant negative association between output and lagged increases in money or credit, as well as between output and interest rate levels, the value and significance of the coefficients were very sensitive to the choice of the sample period and other equation idiosyncrasies. One

---

[33]M2 also includes foreign exchange deposits with domestic banks; arrears are total interenterprise arrears as estimated by the authors based on available (partial) information.

[34]Only in the case of M2 did it turn out to be significantly different from zero, for reasons that remain to be investigated (one possibility being that during most of the sample period domestic inflation was instantaneously reflected in exchange rate depreciation and thus into an increase of the value of the foreign exchange component of M2).

[35]See, for instance, Fischer (1993) or Chart 22 in IMF (1994b).

[36]This point is made by Delpla and Wyplosz (1995).

factor casting serious doubts on any results obtained in such regressions is that economy-wide value added is mismeasured by officially recorded gross industrial output, which constitutes a shrinking portion of the overall production of goods and services. Another important caveat is that the decline in the output of some items may not have a commensurate negative impact on welfare.

While econometrics does not deliver a clear-cut verdict, it does not invalidate the presumption that given the largely inevitable output decline associated with the structural transformation involved with the move to a market economy, lax financial policies overwhelmingly translate into higher inflation and imports rather than into higher production.

Leads, Lags, and Synergies in Structural Reforms

Duality has taken on a new identity: the heavy versus light industry dichotomy of the Soviet period has been replaced by what could be called the "survivalist" versus "subsidized" delineation. Survivalists have emerged in response to price liberalization, the slashing of subsidies and other financial transfers, the advent of positive real interest rates, and privatization.[37] The subsidized have remained in that condition because either they have not been allowed to change—many military firms were not part of the privatization process, restrictions still exist on the sale of land—or lobbying has been perceived as being more beneficial than restructuring. While a significant portion of survivalists use their energies to make profit via product development, marketing, lowering costs, and improving quality, another portion use force to maintain monopoly power. The latter's importance is one sign that the legal and institutional underpinnings of a stable market economy are not as yet in place.

Leads

Price liberalization and administrative price adjustments, exchange rate unification, and privatization constituted the first stage in Russia's sequencing of reform measures. On January 2, 1992, controls on many prices were removed and the remaining administrative prices were increased several-fold. Additional liberalization occurred in March 1992. Now, most domestic prices—except

for natural gas, electricity, water, telephone service, and intercity transportation—are free of direct federal intervention. Local authorities, however, control municipal transport prices and public housing rents and have the right to regulate other consumer prices.[38] In addition, in 1992 and 1993, many enterprises considered to be monopolies faced a maximum profitability markup of 25 percent (this rule elapsed in early 1994). Also, local authorities have imposed regional export quotas for agricultural products in an attempt to increase the availability of those goods on local markets. Yet it is difficult to estimate to what extent local authorities have enforced such measures.

The exchange system was liberalized in 1992. Commercial bank participation in foreign exchange auctions was widened early in the year, the exchange system was virtually unified in July, and current account convertibility was formally introduced for residents in November, when the new foreign exchange law was passed. With the unification of the exchange system, the effective taxation of exports was greatly reduced. In 1993, further growth of the interbank market and greater nonresident access to that market increased the openness of the Russian economy.[39]

Privatization in Russia effectively began in 1987 with the Soviet Law on State Enterprises, which transferred control of enterprises from the ministries and local governments to enterprise managers. The law opened the way for Russian enterprises to engage in *nomenklatura* privatization, a process by which enterprise managers transfer valuable property, structures, and equipment to themselves or their business partners by leasing portions of the original enterprise at giveaway prices.[40]

Dissatisfied with nomenklatura privatization and mistrustful of the ability of federal ministries and local authorities to manage state assets well, reformers in 1992 initiated privatization via auctions of or tender offers for small retail establishments and most medium-sized enterprises (mainly owned by municipalities);[41] employee buyouts and voucher

---

[37]While survivalists may also receive subsidies, they are still characterized by the extent to which they have altered their behavior to find new markets, clients, products, and input combinations.

[38]See IMF (1993) and (1995a) and Koen and Phillips (1993).

[39]See IMF (1993) and (1995a) and Koen and Meyermans (1994).

[40]As of September 1991, leased enterprises (often associated with *nomenklatura* privatization) employed 6½ percent of the Soviet labor force.

[41]Small enterprises are defined as having fewer than 200 employees and a January 1, 1992 book value of fixed assets smaller than rub 1 million; medium-sized enterprises as having between 200 and 1,000 employees or fewer than 200 employees but a book value of fixed assets between Rub 1 million and Rub 50 million; and large enterprises as having more than 1,000 employees or a book value exceeding Rub 50 million.

auctions (the so-called mass privatization) of some medium-sized enterprises and most large enterprises;[42] the monitored sale of shares in the largest firms to strategic foreign investors; the sale of apartments to the current tenants at very favorable terms; and the establishment of private farms. In addition, in late 1994 a large number of enterprises in the defense sector, which previously had been excluded from privatization, became eligible.

Approximately 130,000 enterprises have been privatized or leased with a purchase option through late 1994, which represents over half of the 250,000 state and municipal enterprises that were operating at the beginning of 1992. Most privatized enterprises have been small trade and service enterprises, with three fourths of such enterprises already privatized. About 70 percent of those enterprises were purchased by members of workers' collectives, who enjoyed significantly concessional terms. In addition, about one million completely new small private businesses have been registered.

Privatization through voucher auctions started in December 1992. By mid-1994, 13,500 enterprises, employing more than 16 million workers, had been privatized in this manner, and an estimated 40 million Russians were stockholders in joint-stock companies or in investment funds.

Privatization of housing and farms has also made progress. By late 1994, almost one third of all apartments had been privatized (Table 4.1), most of which were given to tenants at no cost. Existing land legislation permits the private ownership of land for farming, and about 279,000 private farms had been created as of late 1994 covering 11.9 million hectares (or 5 percent of agricultural land).

The gradual tightening of budget constraints was effected through various channels. Privatization, competition from imports, and the cutback of financial transfers played an important role. Also effective were the disruption of traditional supplier and distribution relationships and the arrears crises, as well as the sequestration of government expenditures in late 1993 and 1994. Many enterprises had to look for new solutions to survive—they simply did not have the resources to wait for the Government to bail them out.

Just as significant has been institution building, which has gone a long way in helping Russia surmount its inherited disadvantages. Russian authorities have gradually been gaining control over public finances. One way this came about was with the demise of most of the ruble area and the emergence of new currencies in most neighboring countries. Furthermore, and although it involved a tortuous political process, the independence of

regions has been curtailed with the adoption of the new constitution. In addition, in April 1994, a new formula-based system of effecting financial tax and subsidy transfers between the center and regions was introduced. This may lessen some of the bargaining between the center and regions, which earlier led to higher federal deficits.

Russia also is no longer an isolated country. Especially since 1991, endless waves of technical assistance teams have provided advice on the creation of a market-oriented legal system; on revamping the tax structure; on introducing indirect monetary policy instruments; on the setup of bodies and rules to regulate banks, investment funds, commodity exchanges, and other financial organizations and to promote foreign direct investment; and on ways to improve the payments and settlement system. A fair amount of this advice has been followed, which is bringing Russia's legal and financial infrastructure closer to international norms.

Lags

Russia has a long history, partly due to sheer size, of being a country where the difference between theory and practice has been enormous. Along this vein, modern Russia has lagged most glaringly in the implementation of the plethora of laws, decrees, and regulations that have been enacted. Property rights legislation, bankruptcy laws, and land reform decrees exist but have not been applied sufficiently widely and consistently to yield any consensus concerning their practical content. Weak implementation has been paralleled by jurisdictional conflicts that have resulted in outright confusion as to which laws have precedence, especially with regard to taxation and property rights. Finally, Russian federal and local authorities have not as yet become convinced of the inviolability of contracts. For instance, agreements concerning foreign direct investment have been broken repeatedly. Such a legal nightmare has discouraged investment of all types and hindered the restructuring of enterprises.

The authorities have not as yet developed comprehensive programs for the relocation and retraining of people in the Northern Territories and single-enterprise towns, which are required to address the root causes of the perennial subsidization of these areas, nor has a coherent strategy guided military conversion. In fact, until recently, many defense-related enterprises were in a no-win never-never land: they were not allowed to attract outside investors, and at the same time, they were manufacturing products for some governmental agency for which they were only being paid, if at all, with great delays.

---

[42] For details, see Boycko, Shleifer, and Vishny (1995).

Even the privatization process, which deserves high praise for wresting control of property away from ministerial bureaucrats, has primarily succeeded in transferring ownership and power to managers and employees (with the balance clearly tilted toward managers). While this may diminish incentives for asset stripping, vesting too much control with insiders can slow down enterprise reform.[43] Indeed, incumbent managers were often selected for their ability to lobby for credits or inputs, or because of their position in the Communist Party hierarchy. These skills are obviously less relevant once restructuring, cost cutting, and marketing become the key challenges. Partly because outsiders have insufficient influence in corporate decision making, the transfer of property titles so far has stimulated only meager inflows of new capital. Moreover, the efficiency gains expected from privatization are limited by the large measure of control local governments retain over the use of real estate.

Finally, opportunities for corruption expanded owing to the slow or incomplete liberalization of economic activity.[44] For instance, price liberalization without fully removing quantitative controls on domestic and foreign trade, combined with privileged access to certain resources and markets, may encourage criminal networks to enlarge their control over the economy. In the Soviet period, when a totalitarian government was in place, the criminal portion of the shadow economy was kept in check. Since the demise of the union and in the ensuing regulatory and jurisdictional chaos, a private sector that is part entrepreneurial and part criminal has emerged.

Synergies

Some economists have argued that optimal sequencing of policies should feature structural and institutional change as prior conditions for macrostabilization, involving, for example, the demonopolization and privatization of domestic trade before the liberalization of prices. However, as Berg (1994), discussing Poland, aptly put it, macroeconomic reform to some extent causes structural adjustment. Moreover, abstract arguments about optimal sequencing often ignore some of the real world constraints facing policymakers: price liberalization or exchange rate unification can be decreed overnight, while implementing privatization and bankruptcies is by necessity a drawn-out process. If reformers want to use their political window of opportunity wisely, they should press ahead with those measures that can be promptly executed. Finally, a considerable measure of stabilization has been achieved in several transition economies (e.g., the Baltics and Albania) notwithstanding lagging structural reforms.

Structural reforms and stabilization are most often complements. Delaying the latter is likely to postpone the former, insofar as it means that hard budget constraints are slower to become the rule. Any attempt at gradualism on the macroeconomic front will encourage enterprises to continue to lobby for subsidies in various guises rather than to change their way of doing business and their product mix. Stabilization further diminishes relative price uncertainty and the deadweight losses entailed when agents devote time and energy to protect themselves against the inflation tax. If perceived as sustainable and combined with structural reforms, stabilization improves the investment climate (not least for foreign investors) and thus growth prospects. In particular, it puts in motion reverse capital flight, thus broadening the pool of domestic savings. In sum, insufficient stabilization impedes structural progress.

Admittedly, there may sometimes be tension between structural reform and stabilization objectives. For example, reform of the archaic Russian financial system is eroding the inflation tax base. So far, the sluggishness of the settlement system has sustained transactions demand. The limited availability of alternative financial assets outside large cities also has bolstered money demand. However, the modern technologies that are being put in place, and inflation as it forces agents to learn cash management techniques, cause a ceteris paribus rise in velocity. But even this type of interaction could be interpreted as a case of synergy, to the extent that here structural progress reduces the scope for one of the most inequitable forms of taxation and forces policymakers to move more rapidly to a more desirable tax mix.

Russia has achieved significant progress in spite of the relatively slow movement toward macroeconomic stabilization. Structural reforms have been mutually reinforcing, and budget constraints have gradually hardened for a substantial portion of the economy. The liberalization of foreign trade and the general opening up of the economy have acted both as an antimonopoly device and as a stimulus for more rapid adjustment among survivalist firms, all the more as the real exchange rate appreciation accompanying the move toward positive real interest rates rendered import competition increasingly fierce.

---

[43] As stressed by Shleifer and Vasiliev (1994).

[44] Corruption is not new, however. As emphasized by Gerschenkron (1962), it was widespread in late nineteenth century Russia. It was also pervasive, albeit less conspicuous, under the Soviet regime.

Conclusions

As the upsurge in inflation in the fall of 1994 attested, it is too early to describe Russia's transition as a success story. Nonetheless, much has been achieved since late 1991, especially in the structural area, and while financial stabilization has so far proved elusive, hyperinflation has been avoided.

The collapse in officially recorded output was largely inevitable and has by no means had a commensurate negative impact on welfare.[45] At the same time, if macroeconomic stability could have been attained earlier, domestic and foreign investment in Russia would likely have been much higher, and the economic transformation would have been more deeply grounded than it is now.

Financial stabilization is becoming increasingly difficult insofar as repeated failure has hurt the authorities' credibility, which was never impressive

in the first place. In the meantime, agents are learning how to cope with high open inflation, thus making disinflation harder. On the other hand, the painful lessons from high inflation in Russia and in neighboring countries are also being learned, implying that there may now be more of a consensus on the merits of conventional economic wisdom in this area.

Even on the structural side, progress, while genuine, has been very uneven. Privatization has moved ahead very fast, but enterprise behavior and the business environment, in general, have not improved in tandem. Some firms are adjusting energetically and stand a chance to survive and prosper in the longer run, but others continue to rely too heavily on rent seeking and state subsidies.

As behavioral change still has a long way to go in some sectors and regions, and in light of political uncertainties, the transition process will likely remain chaotic and somewhat unpredictable for some time. But if muddling through may not sound ex ante like an appealing strategy, it is, ex post, far from the worst outcome.

---

[45]In this regard, the situation is much bleaker in some of the other countries of the former Soviet Union.

References

Berg, Andrew, "Does Macroeconomic Reform Cause Structural Adjustment? Lessons from Poland," *Journal of Comparative Economics*, Vol. 18 (June 1994), pp. 376–409.

Boycko, Maxim, Andrei Shleifer, and Robert Vishny, *Privatizing Russia* (Cambridge: MIT Press, 1995).

Brau, Eduard, "External Financial Assistance to the Baltic States, Russia, and Other States of the Former Soviet Union: The Record and the Issues," paper presented at the Conference on Marketization of the Former Soviet Union organized by the Adam Smith Institute held in London on October 26–27, 1994.

Christensen, Benedicte Vibe, *The Russian Federation in Transition: External Developments*, IMF Occasional Paper, No. 111 (Washington: International Monetary Fund, February 1994).

Delpla, Jacques, and Charles Wyplosz, "Russia's Transition: Muddling-Through," in *Russian Economic Reform at Risk*, ed. by Anders Åslund (London: Pinter Publishers, 1995), pp. 19–52.

Easterly, William, and Paolo Vieira da Cunha, "Financing the Storm: Macroeconomic Crisis in Russia," *Economics of Transition*, Vol. 2 (1994), pp. 443–465.

Fischer, Stanley, "The Role of Macroeconomic Factors in Growth," *Journal of Monetary Economics*, Vol. 32 (December 1993), pp. 485–512.

———, "Prospects for Russian Stabilization in the Summer of 1993," in *Economic Transformation in Russia*, ed. by Anders Åslund (London: Pinter Publishers, 1994), pp. 8–25.

Gavrilenkov, Evgeny, and Vincent Koen, "How Large Was the Output Collapse in Russia? Alternative Estimates and Welfare Implications," IMF Working Paper, WP/94/154 (Washington: International Monetary Fund, December 1994).

Gerschenkron, Alexander, *Economic Backwardness in Historical Perspective, A Book of Essays* (Cambridge: Belknap Press of Harvard University Press, 1962).

Grossman, Gregory, "The Underground Economy in Russia," *International Economic Insights*, Vol. 4 (November-December 1993), pp. 14–17.

Hernández-Catá, Ernesto, "Russia and the IMF: The Political Economy of Macro-Stabilization," *Problems of Post-Communism*, Vol. 41 (May–June 1995), pp. 20–27.

International Monetary Fund, *Russian Federation*, Economic Review (Washington: April 1992).

———, *Russian Federation*, IMF Economic Reviews, No.8 (Washington: June 1993).

———(1994a), *Financial Relations Among Countries of the Former Soviet Union*, IMF Economic Reviews, No. 1 (Washington: February 1994).

———(1994b), *World Economic Outlook*, World Economic and Financial Surveys (Washington: October 1994).

———(1995a), *Russian Federation*, IMF Economic Reviews, No. 16 (Washington: March 1995).

———(1995b), "Eastern Europe—Factors Underlying the Weakening Performance of Tax Revenues," in *Economic Systems*, Vol. 19 (June 1995), pp. 23–46.

———, World Bank, Organization for Economic Cooperation and Development and European Bank for Reconstruction and Development, *A Study of the Soviet Economy*, Vol. 1 (Washington: February 1991).

Keynes, John Maynard, *A Short View of Russia* (London: Hogarth Press, 1925).

Koen, Vincent, and Eric Meyermans, "Exchange Rate Determinants in Russia: 1992–93," IMF Working Paper, WP/94/66 (Washington: International Monetary Fund, June 1994).

Koen, Vincent, and Steven Phillips, *Price Liberalization in Russia: Behavior of Prices, Household Incomes and Consumption During the First Year*, Occasional Paper, No. 104 (Washington: International Monetary Fund, June 1993).

Nagy, Piroska, "Muddling Through Economic Chaos: Russia's Financial Policies Since the Start of the Transformation," in *Economic Reforms in Russia: The Early Record and Prospects*, ed. by Mario I. Blejer (San Francisco: International Center for Economic Growth, 1995).

Odling-Smee, John, and Henri Lorie, "The Economic Reform Process in Russia," IMF Working Paper, WP/93/55 (Washington: International Monetary Fund, July 1993).

Odling-Smee, John, and Thomas Wolf, "Economic Reforms in Transition Economies: A Macroeconomic Perspective on the Baltic States, Russia and Other Countries of the Former Soviet Union," mimeo, presented at the seminar on Economic Reform in Russia and Other Economies in Transition: Issues and Prospects held in Moscow on October 18–19, 1994.

Petrakov, Nikolay, "Macroeconomic Regulation of the Market in Russia: Intermediate Results and New Possibilities," mimeo, presented at the seminar on Economic Reform in Russia and Other Economies in Transition: Issues and Prospects held in Moscow on October 18–19, 1994.

Shleifer, Andrei and Dmitry Vasiliev, "Management Ownership and the Russian Privatization," paper presented at the World Bank Conference on Corporate Governance in Central Europe and Russia held in Washington on December 15–16, 1994.

Sokolnikov, Grigoriy Yakovlevich, *New Financial Policy: On the Path to a Hard Currency* (Moscow: Science, 1991) (In Russian).

Tanzi, Vito, "Fiscal Policy and the Economic Restructuring of Economies in Transition," IMF Working Paper, WP/93/22 (Washington: International Monetary Fund, March 1993).

Vavilov, Andrey P., and Oleg V. Vyugin, "The Financial Situation of the Soviet Economy Through the Prism of the Income of the Population and Enterprises," *Economic Systems*, Vol. 15 (October 1991), pp. 195–209.

Wolf, Thomas A., "Currency Arrangements in Countries of the Former Ruble Area and Conditions for Sound Monetary Policy," IMF Paper on Policy Analysis and Assessment, PPAA/94/15 (Washington: International Monetary Fund, July 1994).

World Bank, *Russian Economic Reform, Crossing the Threshold of Structural Change* (Washington: September 1992).

Recent Occasional Papers of the International Monetary Fund

127. Road Maps of the Transition: The Baltics, the Czech Republic, Hungary, and Russia, by Tapio O. Saavalainen, Biswajit Banerjee, Mark S. Lutz, Thomas Krueger, Vincent Koen, and Michael Marrese. 1995.

126. The Adoption of Indirect Instruments of Monetary Policy, by a Staff Team headed by William E. Alexander, Tomás J.T. Baliño, and Charles Enoch and comprising Francesco Caramazza, George Iden, David Marston, Johannes Mueller, Ceyla Pazarbasioglu, Marc Quintyn, Matthew Saal, and Gabriel Sensenbrenner.

125. United Germany: The First Five Years—Performance and Policy Issues, by Robert Corker, Robert A. Feldman, Karl Habermeier, Hari Vittas, and Tessa van der Willigen. 1995.

124. Saving Behavior and the Asset Price "Bubble" in Japan: Analytical Studies, edited by Ulrich Baumgartner and Guy Meredith. 1995.

123. Comprehensive Tax Reform: The Colombian Experience, edited by Parthasarathi Shome. 1995.

122. Capital Flows in the APEC Region, edited by Mohsin S. Khan and Carmen M. Reinhart. 1995.

121. Uganda: Adjustment with Growth, 1987–94, by Robert L. Sharer, Hema R. De Zoysa, and Calvin A. McDonald. 1995.

120. Economic Dislocation and Recovery in Lebanon, by Sena Eken, Paul Cashin, S. Nuri Erbas, Jose Martelino, and Adnan Mazarei. 1995.

119. Singapore: A Case Study in Rapid Development, edited by Kenneth Bercuson with a staff team comprising Robert G. Carling, Aasim M. Husain, Thomas Rumbaugh, and Rachel van Elkan. 1995.

118. Sub-Saharan Africa: Growth, Savings, and Investment, by Michael T. Hadjimichael, Dhaneshwar Ghura, Martin Mühleisen, Roger Nord, and E. Murat Uçer. 1995.

117. Resilience and Growth Through Sustained Adjustment: The Moroccan Experience, by Saleh M. Nsouli, Sena Eken, Klaus Enders, Van-Can Thai, Jörg Decressin, and Filippo Cartiglia, with Janet Bungay. 1995.

116. Improving the International Monetary System: Constraints and Possibilities, by Michael Mussa, Morris Goldstein, Peter B. Clark, Donald J. Mathieson, and Tamim Bayoumi. 1994.

115. Exchange Rates and Economic Fundamentals: A Framework for Analysis, by Peter B. Clark, Leonardo Bartolini, Tamim Bayoumi, and Steven Symansky. 1994.

114. Economic Reform in China: A New Phase, by Wanda Tseng, Hoe Ee Khor, Kalpana Kochhar, Dubravko Mihaljek, and David Burton. 1994.

113. Poland: The Path to a Market Economy, by Liam P. Ebrill, Ajai Chopra, Charalambos Christofides, Paul Mylonas, Inci Otker, and Gerd Schwartz. 1994.

112. The Behavior of Non-Oil Commodity Prices, by Eduardo Borensztein, Mohsin S. Khan, Carmen M. Reinhart, and Peter Wickham. 1994.

111. The Russian Federation in Transition: External Developments, by Benedicte Vibe Christensen. 1994.

110. Limiting Central Bank Credit to the Government: Theory and Practice, by Carlo Cottarelli. 1993.

109. The Path to Convertibility and Growth: The Tunisian Experience, by Saleh M. Nsouli, Sena Eken, Paul Duran, Gerwin Bell, and Zühtü Yücelik. 1993.

108. Recent Experiences with Surges in Capital Inflows, by Susan Schadler, Maria Carkovic, Adam Bennett, and Robert Kahn. 1993.

107. China at the Threshold of a Market Economy, by Michael W. Bell, Hoe Ee Khor, and Kalpana Kochhar with Jun Ma, Simon N'guiamba, and Rajiv Lall. 1993.

106. Economic Adjustment in Low-Income Countries: Experience Under the Enhanced Structural Adjustment Facility, by Susan Schadler, Franek Rozwadowski, Siddharth Tiwari, and David O. Robinson. 1993.

105. The Structure and Operation of the World Gold Market, by Gary O'Callaghan. 1993.

104. Price Liberalization in Russia: Behavior of Prices, Household Incomes, and Consumption During the First Year, by Vincent Koen and Steven Phillips. 1993.

Note: For information on the title and availability of Occasional Papers not listed, please consult the IMF Publications Catalog or contact IMF Publication Services.